The Secret of Mill Creek Raceway

By

Becky Coelho

The Secret of Mill Creek Raceway

Other works by Becky Coelho

"Born In December" © 2006
"Through The Crystal" © 2007
"It Doesn't Always Show On The Outside" © 2009
"Building Dominoes" © 2009

ISBN: 978-0-557-18086-8

Printed by: Lulu.com

A very special Thanks to Adam Fanning, my cover model

Chapter 1

The trees are just starting to turn which to Sally seemed early. But then Sally couldn't wrap her brain around the fact that it is the middle of October. Autumn has always been her favorite time of year. She loves the absence of humidity, the bringing in of the harvest, the cool nights, the first smells of fireplaces, no more air conditioners buzzing and more people taking walks in the neighborhood. Sally Cooper sat on the front porch waving to all the neighbors as they passed by and that's when she noticed him.

He was tall, tan and muscular. His jeans were pulled tight since he had one boot on the second step leading to Hal Graves' porch. His flannel shirt was also pulled tight across his back as he leaned on the porch rail while he and Hal carried on a conversation. Hal's hands were flying as if he were speaking in sign. Neighbors always teased Hal that he couldn't talk if his hands were tied. The cool fall breeze blew his light brown hair off his brow. Sally couldn't see his face, but she just knew he was handsome.

Vic came out of the house with a hot cup of cider for her and sat on the top step next to her.

"Thanks, honey," Sally said as she took a sip of the sweet hot brew not taking her eyes off the new stranger.

"You know who he is, Mom?" Vic asked his mother. Sally shook her head. Sally's twelve year old son usually knew everything that went on in their small Midwest town of Payson, Illinois. She was really surprised he didn't start spewing an encyclopedia's worth on this guy. Vic set his empty cider cup down on the porch, hopped down to the sidewalk and started up the street toward Hal's house.

"Where you going?" Sally asked even though she didn't need to. Vic waved at her and kept on walking. Sally watched as he crossed the street and walked over to the gray bungalow at the corner of Washington and Edwards Streets. Vic was like the proverbial fly on the wall. People saw him, but he was just a part of the scenery. When he arrived at Hal's, he simply climbed up the steps, not disturbing the conversation and sat on the porch swing.

"So what am I supposed to do until spring?" The stranger asked Hal.

"Well, we'll pull her out and get her fixed up and ready to race," Hal said getting so excited. "You want to walk back and take a look at her?" The stranger nodded.

Hal grabbed his cane and slowly walked down the steps. Vic jumped up and hopped over the porch rail and followed the two men to the back yard to the garage. Hal pulled out a bundle of keys from his pocket, hung his cane on his arm as he found the silver key to the garage. He carried the cane the remainder of the way holding the key as if it were the key to the prize.

"I haven't been back here for a couple weeks," Hal said inserting the key in the door knob. He slowly turned the knob. The sun shone on the shiny black something in there as Hal opened the door. Vic was trying to see even though he had seen it hundreds of times before. Hal reached in and hit the button to open the big door. Slowly it opened. The reflection off the polished chrome of the engine blinded Vic and he moved over a bit to get out of the light.

"Well, Adam, what do you think of her?" Hal asked the young man standing in front of the black beauty 350 stock with his hands on his hips.

Adam let out of wolf whistle before walking a little closer to the car. He seemed to be afraid to get too close to the wondrous machine. He shook his head as he walked around the back, looking inside and coming back out in front of the car. The engine was spotless. It looked as though it had just come off the assembly line. Adam leaned in and took a good look.

Adam pulled back from the car and let the hood down with a thud wiping away any trace of smudge or fingerprints with his shirt sleeve.

"So what do you want to do to her?" Adam asked once again looking at the beautiful car. "She looks ready for the track."

"There's some stuff I want to do," Hal said. "I got a guy coming to bring her up to snuff…if you know what I'm saying."

"Well, Hal, this isn't going to be a forty hour a week job," Adam said. "I'm going to need something else to keep me busy all winter around here. Just looking around, I don't think I'm going to find much to do in the line of a job."

"Well, have you ever driven combines, semis?" Hal asked. "We can keep you busy pretty much til Christmas with the harvest around here."

"That takes care of almost three months," Adam said. "What happens after that?"

Adam was looking out for himself. He was not the kind of guy that mooched off of others and wanted to have money in his hand to pay his own way. He was the middle child of a family of seven children and the family pinched pennies just to have food on the table and clothes on their backs. Adam was lucky that he was the oldest boy. His clothes were new to him, even though they were garage sale or thrift store bought. His sisters wore hand me downs until they were in threads. No, sir, Adam wanted to have the cash at the ready to be able to pay for what he needed.

"What are you going to need money for anyway?" Hal asked the young man. "You can live here with me. I've got plenty of room and I'm pretty quiet. You keep the house clean for me and that'll take care of your room."

"Yeah, and you'll be on me constantly about the car." Adam said shaking his head. "I don't think so. I'd rather not live with my boss. No offense."

"None taken," Hal said. "But, you know, since my wife passed some six years ago, it does get pretty lonely. I do get tired of eating meals by myself. I don't like to go out to eat by myself. And I have had just about all the TV dinners I care to recollect." Hal paused. He walked over to close the garage door so they could head back to the house. Then he stopped, turned around and looked at Adam. "But, I understand. A strapping young buck like you might want a place you can bring ladies to. You know, that wouldn't bother me either. When I take my hearing aid out, I'm deaf as a rock."

Hal laughed as he reached in to push the button to close the big garage door. Then he pulled the smaller door closed and locked it. Hal looked at Adam who was smiling at the old man. Hal winked at him as they started toward the house.

"Let me give it some thought, Hal," Adam said. "I've never lived with anyone since I left home."

"Where you staying tonight?" Hal asked him as he climbed the porch steps and sat down on his rocking chair.

“Hadn’t given it any thought yet,” Adam said. “Is there a motel in town?”

“Well, there is,” Hal said looking over at Vic before continuing. “I wouldn’t recommend it. They rent the rooms by the hour, if you get my meaning.” Adam nodded.

“Well, I might just go back to the city and find a place and maybe some work,” Adam said running his fingers through his hair on the top of his head. As he did so, the soft hair fell back into place across his forehead just above his ears. He knew it was at least twelve miles back to Quincy and he didn’t have a ride since he had hitched a ride out with the pastor of the Congregational Church earlier in the day. He looked toward the northwest, the direction of Quincy.

“You can take my old Taurus if you want,” Hal said. “I’ll even make you a deal. If I give you my grocery list and some money, you can do my shopping for me and let me know your decision about staying with me when you bring my groceries and the car back in a couple a days.”

There went that hand again to the top of Adam’s head pushing the hair off of his brow. He thought about Hal’s deal for a few seconds.

“All right,” Adam said walking up the porch steps. “Let’s get that list wrote so I can get into town before it gets too late and I can’t find a place to stay.”

“I’ll tell you a nice place to stay,” Hal said as he got up to go into the house. “There’s a nice little place called Althoff’s out North 24th Street. Ain’t nothing fancy, but they are good people and it is reasonable. Go just past the Red Cross and it’s on the left.”

When they got to the kitchen, Adam wrote items on a list as Hal walked around the kitchen yelling out different things he needed from the grocery store. There were more things than just TV dinners, too. Hal was ordering things to prepare big meals.

“I thought you didn’t care about cooking,” Adam said as he wrote down things like flour, sugar and several different spices.

“Didn’t say I don’t mind it. Make sure you get McCormick spices.” Hal said. “They’re always fresher. And go to HyVee. Their employees will help you if you can’t find something. It’s true what they say, you know.” Then Hal sang the company’s jingle, “There’s a helpful smile in every aisle.”

Adam smiled at him as he wrote down the additional orders. When the list was done, Hal handed the car keys to his 2002 Taurus and a hundred dollar bill for the groceries to Adam.

"Oh, the old gal might need gas," Hal said adding an additional $50 before handing it over to the young man. "You got enough money for the motel?" He asked Adam then.

"Yeah, I'll be all right for a while," Adam said as he stuffed the cash in his front pocket.

When the two men were walking back toward the garage once again, Hal was explaining about the key ring that Adam was holding. It was also the remote for the garage door for the side where the Taurus was hidden. Just as the door was opening, Vic came running around the side of the house carrying Adam's backpack that he retrieved from beside the porch steps. Sometimes he was noticed and came in handy from time to time. Adam took the pack from the boy and tossed it into the car without a word.

"Thanks Hal," Adam said. "I'll call you and let you know when I'll be back. It'll be a day or two. I want to see the job situation before I make any decisions. You understand."

Hal nodded and extended his hand to Adam who took it. Hal didn't wish any bad luck on the young man, but he was hoping he would be back in a day or two to stay. He liked him and he thought they could work well together. Adam got in the car and headed toward town. Vic tapped Hal on the arm.

"What is it, boy?" Hal asked as he turned in Vic's direction as if he just now noticed he was there.

"Why didn't you suggest that he stay in Mom's apartment? It's empty right now," Vic said looking up at the old man.

"Damn, I never gave it a thought," Hal said walking back to the house. "Why didn't you bring it up?"

"I'm not supposed to interrupt," Vic said remembering that he had been told several times when he was younger by adults, including Hal, not to interrupt their conversations. Hal just looked at him and smiled.

Chapter 2

Adam had no trouble finding the Althoff Motel and pulled into the parking lot. He got a room for just one night. On the way to the motel he had stopped to buy a newspaper and supper at a Subway he passed along the way. Adam opened the paper to the Jobs section as he mindlessly ate his sandwich.

There were a lot of openings for semi truck drivers. He could do that until April. But, would he be home enough to help Hal with the car? There were the usual sales jobs, nursing jobs and professional jobs. Actually there weren't too many jobs at all. Adam finished his sandwich and threw the wrapper and napkin toward the trash can, missing by just an inch.

"Damn," he said as he got up to pick it up and throw it away. He picked up the newspaper a second time. He had glanced over an ad for a school custodian. He could do that as long as he didn't throw things and miss. Wow, it was in Payson, too, right across the street from Hal's house. He would get Hal's groceries early in the morning and head out to Payson to talk to Hal about that job so he could be there right when school starts. Adam threw the paper on the table, walked over to turn on the television but instead pulled out Hal's card and sat on the bed. It wasn't too late to call him now.

"Hal, it's Adam," he said when Hal answered the phone. "I saw an ad in the paper about a job out your way that might hold me over the winter. Wondered if you knew anything about it."

"What job is that?" Hal asked as he turned the volume down on Leno.

"It says that the school is looking for a custodian," Adam said getting comfortable on the bed and kicking his boots off.

"I swear I'm getting more forgetful in my old age," Hal said. "Sure I know about that. They hired a young guy and he was standing around watching the kids mostly. Found out he liked kids, if you catch my meaning. So they let him go as soon as they found that out. Even called the law on him. But now they need someone like yesterday."

"I could do that," Adam said hoping and saying a silent prayer he could get the job.

"You don't like kids, do you?" Hal asked him.

"They're all right, I guess," Adam said. "But they'll be in class most of the time, won't they?"

"That's not what I mean," Hal said.

"Oh," Adam cried once he figured out the question. "Oh, no man, I'm not like that. If it were up to me, I wouldn't a called the law on that guy. I would a taken him to a remote holler and…well; let's just say he wouldn't a done anything to any more kids."

"I totally agree with you there, son," Hal said with a little laugh. "Let me call Jim right now and see if he can see you in the morning."

"I'll leave early and pick up your groceries and be out there by 8:00 then," Adam said. "Does that sound all right?"

"You might want to wait until all the kids are in their classes and the busses are tucked away. I'd wait until about 8:30," Hal suggested.

Adam turned on the television to relax and get ready for a good night's sleep. But, he was nervous and excited. It had been over a year since he had a real job. This would be the ideal job for him since he could work during the school year, work on the car at night and race all summer. Maybe he would take Hal up on his offer to live with him. But he really didn't want to live with someone else, especially his boss. That would be the bad thing about working out in Payson. He didn't have a vehicle so he might have to just bite the bullet and move in with the old man.

Adam pointed the remote and turned off the television. It was too early to sleep and he was too excited. When he drove in he noticed there was no restaurant or bar at the motel, and it was quite a way from the center of town. Adam had never been to Quincy before and didn't know where to go to spend a few hours to unwind. He decided to take a walk up to the motel office.

When he walked in the office the same middle aged lady was still there behind the counter.

"Something I can do for you, hon?" She asked looking up from her magazine when the bell jingled on the door when Adam walked in.

"I was just wondering what a guy does here on a Monday night around 9:30," Adam asked as he looked up at the clock to see the time. "I'm just not tired and I've never been here before. I've got a job interview tomorrow and I'm kind of nervous and excited about it."

Adam didn't know why he told her all that. He was usually a much quieter guy. He leaned on the counter and ran his hand through his hair indicating his nervousness.

"Well, hon, all the movies in town have done started," she said. "There's a bowling alley, if you're into that. We've got several bars if you're just into drinking or there're some with pool tables. Don't think there're any bands playing anywhere." She was looking at the ceiling as if she was picking things out of the air. "We've got a Y, but I think it's close to closing time, too. I'm sorry I can't help you more, hon."

"I figure I got started kinda late," Adam said. "I'll just go back and watch TV."

"How are you at playing cards?" She asked Adam as he had one hand on the door.

"Beg your pardon, ma'am?" Adam asked stopped in his tracks looking back over his shoulder.

"Well, I have to sit here until midnight and I've read this magazine about three times," she smiled and pulled out a deck of cards. "I always cheat at Solitaire."

Adam walked back over to the end of the counter, pulling a chair behind him and sat down extending his hand.

"Adam Dieker," he said introducing himself.

"Anna Willer," she said taking Adam's hand. "What's your pleasure?" She asked as she got ready to deal the cards.

"Never played much with just one other person," Adam said. "Our family always played Euchre, Pitch, Poker and such. You name something and I'll let you know if I can play it." Adam flashed his smile and Anna hoped he could play something.

"What about Gin Rummy?" She asked him. Adam nodded and she dealt out the cards.

"So tell me Adam, where you from?" Anna asked him with a sincere interest but also to try to break his train of thought.

"Here and there," Adam said not letting her get the better of him. She put her cards down so he couldn't see them and looked at him.

"Where'd you grow up? Got a home town? Family?" Anna sat and waited until he started talking before she started playing again.

"You writing a book?" He asked as he discarded and smiled.

"I might be," Anna said as she drew a card and immediately discarded a deuce of hearts.

"The travelers through the motel," Adam teased her as he picked up the deuce and discarded.

"Not a bad title," she said as she picked up his discard and laid her cards down. "Gin!"

"Damn!" Adam said as he saw the card he needed on the table in her hand. He picked up the cards and began to shuffle.

"I grew up in Bevier, Missouri," Adam started still shuffling the cards. "I was the middle child of seven. I had three older sisters and two younger brothers and a baby sister. My daddy was a ranger at Long Branch State Park just like his daddy and my momma's daddy. My momma had a day care until my little sister started school and then she was a kindergarten teacher. We went to the Baptist church every Sunday with my grandparents on both sides and my daddy's brothers' families. I never been married and don't have any kids," Adam said as he started dealing looking straight into Anna's bluish gray eyes. "Enough for you?"

"You sound like you had a great childhood and family life," Anna said looking back into Adam's beautiful dreamy brown eyes. "Why do I get the feeling you aren't a happy man?"

"That, my dear, is a long story," Adam plopped the deck of cards between them and picked up his cards. Anna was still looking at him even though she took her first card.

Adam and Anna played cards until almost midnight.

"Well, what's the score?" Adam asked her at 11:45 peeking at the score pad.

"Let's see," Anna said as she was adding up the tally. "Oh damn! Looks like I owe you $3,497." She looked up at him. "Are you willing to have pity on this old widow woman?"

"You wake me up tomorrow morning at 6:00 and we'll call it even," Adam said. "I don't have an alarm clock and I have a big day tomorrow."

"That's a deal," Anna said as she turned around and punched a few buttons on the switch board. "Your wake-up call is entered for 6:00 AM, sir."

"You cheat," Adam laughed at her as he got up to go back to his room. "Thanks for helping me pass the time."

"Thank you, too," Anna said. "I had a quick evening."

Adam waved to her as he passed by the big picture window on his way back to his room. When he entered his room, he went straight to the bathroom to take a shower and get ready to go to bed. Within ten minutes he came back into the room, a towel wrapped around his waist carrying his clothes. Adam threw his clothes on the bed, but then picked up his jeans, folded them neatly and put them on desk. He then picked up his shirt, gave it a brisk shake and hung it on the chair. His underwear and socks were put into a plastic bag and put on the desk next to his jeans. He made sure his boots were put neatly side by side under the chair. Only then did he crawl into bed and turn out the light.

Adam was dreaming about a beautiful woman. He was walking with her in a park. They looked as though they were in love. He was caressing her. He couldn't see her face, but he knew she was very pretty with her long blond hair. He held her close and was just getting ready to kiss her when the phone rang.

The phone brought Adam out of a sound sleep. He had to look around a little before he knew where he was and what sound he was hearing. He reached over and picked up the phone and dropped it back into the receiver. He sat up in bed rubbing his eyes adjusting to the partial darkness. He looked at the clock and it was only 5:50.

"Cute, Anna," Adam said thinking he could have slept ten more minutes and maybe got to kiss the beautiful woman in his dream.

Well, he was awake now. He grabbed his backpack from next to his bed and pulled out some clean underwear and socks. He put them on and turned on the light. He walked to the desk and pulled on his jeans when there was a knock at his door. He quickly zipped his fly before looking out the curtain.

"What the hell are you doing here?" Adam asked Anna when he opened the door running his hand through his hair. She walked in carrying two green bags from Walgreens. Adam grabbed his shirt, pulled it on and buttoned it up as he walked over to the table. Anna set the bags on the table and turned to him.

"I brought breakfast for you," Anna said as she pulled a plate of hot food out of one of the bags. "I didn't know what you liked so I brought a little of everything." And that she did. There were scrambled eggs, sausage, bacon, ham, hashed browns, pancakes, biscuits and gravy. There were two big empty cups and some orange juice and milk. "If you want coffee, we got it in the office."

"Do I look that deprived?" Adam said when he saw the table full of food and sat down.

"You look a might puny," Anna smiled as she sat down and handed him a fork, knife and an empty plate. Adam started to fill his plate and waited until Anna had what she wanted before he bowed his head in silent prayer.

"Thanks so much for doing this," Adam said to Anna. "I won't have to eat for the rest of the day."

"It was the least I could do to get you started off on your new career," Anna said watching the young man enjoy his breakfast.

"Well, it sure is good. You're going to have to tell me where Quincy has such an awesome breakfast buffet. I wouldn't mind taking advantage of this every now and then," Adam said as he shoveled in a mouthful of eggs.

"Well, HyVee has one on the weekend, and I think one of the other motels has one, too," Anna said. "But this came from the Willer kitchen," Anna said with a smile.

"You did?" Adam couldn't finish his sentence with his mouth full but pointed to the table of food with his fork. Anna nodded. Adam shook his head in disbelief and shoveled in another mouthful with a big grin.

When most of the food was gone, Adam washed it down with a big glass of orange juice. He sat back in his chair and patted his flat belly.

"I may have to loosen my belt in order to get up and move," Adam said with a little laugh. "Did I do most of that?" He asked referring to the nearly empty containers of food.

"Yeah, you did," Anna said. "There are a couple pieces of bacon left. You sure you don't want them, too?" Adam shook his head and waved his hand.

"Don't even tease me. I have to go grocery shopping now," Adam said with a horrifying look on his face. "Just the thought of that makes me want to puke." Then realizing what he said, he said, "Sorry."

Adam got up from his chair, put the plastic bag of dirty clothes in the bottom of his backpack, put his wallet in his back pocket and sat on the bed. He pulled on one boot then the other before standing up and smoothing his jeans around his boots.

"Can I help you clean this up?" Adam asked Anna as she was picking up the forks and cups.

"No, I just want the things that aren't disposable," Anna said.

"The maid can take care of the rest."

Adam walked Anna out to her car thanking her again for the great breakfast and asking her for directions to the grocery store. He said he remembered seeing it when he came in last night.

"Hope you get the job, Adam," Anna said as she got in her car.

"Thanks," Adam said as he waved and watched her back out of the parking lot.

Adam pulled up in front of Hal's about 8:15. The school looked pretty quiet and the busses were all parked under the canopy near the highway when Adam made the curve into town. Adam started carrying bags of groceries into Hal's house and putting them on the kitchen table.

"Which ones have anything that needs to go in the fridge or freezer?" Hal asked as Adam felt for coolness on the bottom of the bags. Adam handed him a couple bags and Hal started to empty them. Adam went out to the car for more bags. This time Adam set anything cold on the counter so Hal could take care of them right away. One more trip and Adam had all the bags, plus the gallon of milk in the house. Adam started to empty the bags on the table.

"Leave them," Hal said.

"I got to do something," Adam said. "I can't sit and wait and do nothing."

"Then head over to school and get to work," Hal said smiling at the anxious young man.

"Are you serious?" Adam asked grabbing the back of the old wooden kitchen chair.

"I talked to Jim last night and he said that if I recommended you, that's all he needed," Hal said. Adam was grinning showing off his pearly whites. "Listen hear, boy." The old man grabbed Adam by the forearm. "Don't make me look bad."

"No, sir," Adam said seriously. "Thank you, Hal."

Adam started toward the door and was just about through the living room when he came back to the kitchen.

"You need help putting this stuff away?" Adam asked.

"Get out a here," Hal yelled throwing an empty plastic bag Adam's way.

Adam turned around and ran out the front door, jumped down the four front porch steps and practically bounced over to the school. Hal saw him out the window and limped quickly to the front porch.

"Hey, kid," he yelled. Adam turned around. "It's at the high school." Hal yelled as loud as he could and pointed across the high way toward the larger high school building.

Adam waved at Hal and quickly made the turn and trotted over to the high school.

Chapter 3

Adam walked up the porch steps about 4:30 and smelled something pretty good coming from the inside of Hal's house. When he walked in his mouth was watering from the smell of roast beef and carrots in the oven. He didn't see Hal anywhere and wondered if he had someone else cooking for him. Adam couldn't figure out what the cinnamon smell was but he sure liked that, too.

Adam walked out to the back yard looking for Hal but didn't see him there. The Taurus was right where he left it this morning and he would have to remember to give back the key to Hal. Back in the house, Adam noticed that the bathroom door, as well as both bedroom doors, was open. Then he heard the front door open.

"Hey there," Hal said. "When you get home?" Hal walked across the living room into the kitchen and opened the oven just a bit then closed it quickly.

"Just a minute ago," Adam said. "What have you got in there? It smells great!" Adam pulled a chair out from the table and sat down.

"Just supper," Hal said. "Everything should be ready about a half hour. So tell me about your day." Hal sat down across from Adam.

"Well, it's a job," Adam said. "Cleaning floors and bathrooms mostly. But it pays O.K. and keeps me busy. It's honest pay for honest work. That's all I asked for."

Then Adam remembered Hal's change and car key.

"Oh, here's your receipt and change from this morning," Adam said pulling a receipt and change out of the front pocket of his jeans. "I got gas at the same place and they gave me five cents off a gallon for showing the receipt so here is that receipt." This next part was hard for Adam. "Hal now that I have this job, it really would be kind of stupid to live in Quincy and drive back and forth." Hal stopped him.

"That reminds me. You know the kid that was here yesterday with us," Hal said not as a question. "They live just across the street and down the block. His mom has an upstairs apartment she usually rents out to teachers. It's not rented this year. You interested in that? We'd be close but not together."

"How much does she get for it?" Adam asked. Hal shook his head.

"Let's give her a call and see if you can go over after supper," Hal suggested. Adam nodded. "Speaking of supper, grab some plates out a that cabinet there." Adam obeyed then found the forks, knives, and whatever else Hal ordered him to get to set the table.

"Oh, looky here," Hal said as he pulled a roaster of roast beef, carrots, a couple whole onions and halved potatoes out of the oven and set it on top of the stove. "Take a whiff."

"I've smelled it since I came home," Adam said. "But what is the cinnamon I've been sniffing?"

"Hay, hay," Hal laughed. "That's a secret. It's up in the confectioner's oven. It's one of my favorites this time of year. You'll have to wait for dessert." The old man laughed as he sat down.

"Hello, Hal, how are you?" Sally answered her phone once she knew who was on the other end.

"Hi sweetheart, have you and Vic had dessert yet?" Hal asked her looking over at Adam.

"No, we are just now sitting down to supper," Sally said winking at Vic. He quietly clapped his hands.

"I have a young man who would like to talk to you about your apartment," Hal got to business. "I thought I would bring over dessert and Vic and I could take care of that while you two discuss business."

"Sounds fine to me," Sally said. "When do you want to come?"

"We're just starting to eat, too." Hal looked at Adam. "About half hour or so?" He nodded.

"That sounds fine," Sally said and Vic was thrilled even though he didn't know how soon they were coming.

As soon as the men were finished eating one of the best roast beef dinners Adam said he had ever had, Hal got up and went to the other oven. He put on a pair of oven mitts and pulled out a 9 x 13 baking pan and quickly laid some aluminum foil over it loosely as if he didn't want Adam to see what it was.

"Did you get vanilla ice cream this morning?" Hal asked Adam. He nodded. "Get it out of the freezer and let's get a move on."

"Can you handle that and your cane, too?" Adam asked more out of concern than being nosey to learn what was in the pan.

"Damn," Hal cursed. He flipped off one of the mitts. "Go ahead and put it on." He waited until Adam had the mitt on his hand. "Take it! But, don't you dare peek!" Hal shook off the other mitt and grabbed Adam's other hand and slid the mitt on him. "Don't want you dropping it."

Hal was very slow walking up the street. Adam wondered if he should have driven the short distance. But, they made it and Hal ordered Adam to set the pan on Sally's stove. Vic put the vanilla ice cream in the freezer. He walked back to Hal.

"Is that your famous...?" Vic was silenced when Hal put his hand over the youth's mouth.

"Don't let the cat out a the bag, boy," Hal scolded Vic. The boy nodded with Hal's handed attached.

"Come with me, Adam. We'll let those two fuss," Sally said as she led Adam out the back door of her house. "The entrance to the apartment is actually above our garage. It is just perfect for one person," Sally said as they walked outside.

Sally unlocked a door next to her big garage door which opened to a staircase. At the top was another door that led into a very large room which served as living room, dining room and kitchen. On either side of the kitchen cabinets were doors. One door led into a utility room with a stacked washer and dryer. Through the other door was the bathroom and bedroom. Between the utility room and bathroom was a nice sized closet. The bright apartment was completely furnished including linens, pots and pans, dishes, flatware, and glassware. Sally told Adam that all utilities are furnished except for cable since there is no longer cable TV in Payson.

"We have a tenant," Sally said when she and Adam walked back into the kitchen where Hal and Vic were waiting for them.

"Now?" Ask Vic. Hal nodded as Sally and Adam sat down.

Vic brought over the pan of still warm apple crunch and sat it in the middle of the table. Hal had a big spatula ready to dish up plates for everyone.

"I remember my mom made this for us," Adam said taking a deep breath swallowing the sweet aroma.

"You want ice cream on yours?" Hal asked as he passed a plate to young Vic.

"No thanks, sir. I like mine straight up," Adam laughed as he felt his mouth ready to wrap around a fork full of the dessert.

Adam stuck his fork into the warm crunch and took a bite. He closed his eyes and let the caramel of the brown sugar melt in his mouth. He enjoyed crunching the coating and tasting the apples.

"This brings back so many memories," Adam said. "But I think this is almost better than my mom's."

"Hal used to run the cafeteria over at school," Sally said, bragging on the old man.

"That was another lifetime, girl," Hal said taking a bite of crunch with ice cream.

"So that's why that roast was out of this world," Adam said. "If I stick around you, I'm going to gain weight and not be able to fit in that car."

"Won't let that happen, boy," Hal said. "Speaking of which, walk me back home and get your bag out a the car so you can get settled."

"So what's Sally's story?" Adam asked Hal on the way back to Hal's car.

"Best you ask her about it," Hal said. "If she wants you to know, she'll tell you." Adam nodded.

"What about you, Hal?" Adam asked. "Why did you quit cooking at the school? You aren't that old." Adam helped Hal up the porch steps and Hal sat in his rocker.

"I guess you could say, I got burnt out," Hal said looking over toward the school.

"But you enjoy cooking," Adams said. Hal smiled, got up and started for the door.

"I'll see you tomorrow evening," Hal said. "Come over and help me clean up the leftovers. G'night." With that, Hal walked into the house and closed the door.

Adam grabbed his backpack and walked back to Sally's house. He didn't have a key to the apartment. He knocked on her front door and Vic let him in.

"Your mom home?" Adam asked the boy when Sally walked into the room. "Uh, I didn't get a key."

"Oh, I'm sorry. Let me get it for you," Sally said. "It's in the kitchen." Adam followed her into the kitchen. Vic followed both of them.

"So, you live here all your life?" Adam asked Sally just to break the tense silence.

"No, I moved out here when I married Vic's father," Sally said handing Adam the key.

"I didn't know you were married," Adam said trying to see if Sally was wearing a ring.

"I'm not now," Sally said with a sad tone to her voice. "My husband was in the Army and was sent to Iraq. On his third tour he didn't make it back."

"Hey, I'm real sorry," Adam said. "I didn't mean to bring up sad memories."

"It's been a few years ago now," Sally said looking over to her son. "We're doing OK."

"Do you work at the school, too?" Adam asked as he started walking toward the back door.

"No, I work right next door, at the bank," Sally said pointing out her door.

"That's pretty convenient," Adam said. "Well, good night then." Adam pushed open the screen door and walked out. He saw Vic wave to him from the window. He waved back as he opened the door and walked in.

Adam got settled in his new apartment. It was very comfortable and he could see the entire campus of both the elementary and high schools of Payson Community School District. There was a bunch of kids playing on the ball diamond, a few people walking on the sidewalk in front of the bank and there were some of the members of the cross country track team running on the black top road heading toward the school. Beyond the school lay rolling farm land edged with pastures. The sun was just below the horizon leaving a hint of houses here and there out in the countryside.

Adam hung up his only other pair of jeans…his dress pants…in the closet. He pulled out two plain white t-shirts and placed them in the dresser next to his white boxers and white tube socks. He hung up his other flannel shirt next to his jeans. He had enough clothes for four days before he would have to do laundry as long as he didn't get his jeans too dirty. He just hoped it didn't get too cold before pay day because that was one of the first things he wanted to buy…a jacket. Adam dropped his dirty underwear and socks from the other day right into the washer as that is what he would do tonight with what he had on.

Adam sprawled out across the bed. It felt pretty comfortable. It was plenty long enough for him, had plenty of blankets for him and the pillow was nice and fluffy. Adam thought he was really going to like the apartment, even though there was no television or radio in it.

He reached in to his backpack and pulled out one final item, laid it on the bed before putting the backpack on the top shelf of the closet. Adam walked back over to the bed, picked up the small, old worn Bible and sat back down. His daddy had given it to him when his Grandpa Dieker had passed away going on ten years already. Adam carried the Bible with him and read from it every day. He enjoyed the Psalms and the stories of Jesus in the Gospels. But he read the letters of Paul mostly because he felt Paul was telling him how to live his life. And it showed. The pages of the New Testament were dog eared and stained. Adam even kept the book together with a big rubber band. He turned the book over and over in his hand, looking out the window. It was still too early. He laid it back on the bed and walked toward the kitchen.

He looked in the cabinets seeing all the dishes and such. There were no can goods, nothing to eat. He opened the refrigerator and it was totally empty. Adam pulled his wallet from his pocket and saw he had a few dollars so he decided to walk to the Quick Stop to pick up something for breakfast in the morning.

The street lights were just coming on and the night had taken on a chill. Most of the sidewalks were now empty as were the streets. The town had become very quiet. There was one car at the Quick Stop when Adam walked in the door. He walked back to the cooler and picked up a half gallon of 2% milk before turning down the cereal aisle. There wasn't much to choose from. Adam looked at the prices and understood why most of the boxes were quite dusty. He decided to get a box of Hostess cupcakes instead; at least the date was current on them.

"You Hal's new driver," the clerk commented when Adam went to pay for his items. "$4.83 please."

"Yes, I am," Adam replied thinking that news really traveled fast in this small town; and prices were very high here, too. Adam handed the clerk a five dollar bill and waited quietly for his change.

"You really think he'll get that car going?" The clerk asked handing Adam his change.

"Don't know," Adam said. "I just saw the outside of it." Adam pocketed the change and turned toward the door. “Thanks,” he said as he pushed the door and stepped outside.

“Hope he does,” the clerk said. “It’d be nice to have a winner from Payson again.”

Adam barely heard the last comment but it was enough to put pressure on him. He hadn’t been there twenty-four hours and already people knew who he was and what was expected of him. He walked quickly back to his apartment to get out of the chill of the night.

Adam put the milk in the refrigerator and the cupcakes on top. He decided a good shower would make him warm and then he’d hit the sack for the night. The shower did feel good, but there was no soap. Oh well, he’d have to get some tomorrow.

The hot shower not only warmed up Adam’s body but it also warmed up his bedroom. He walked out with the towel wrapped around his waist. He picked up the Bible and went to his knees next to his bed. The Bible fell open to the thirteenth chapter of Hebrews. Adam folded his hands over the Bible and closed his eyes. He didn’t have to read the chapter, he knew it by heart

> “Keep on loving one another as brothers and sisters. Do not forget to show hospitality to strangers, for by so doing some people have shown hospitality to angels without knowing it. Continue to remember those in prison as if you were together with them in prison, and those who are mistreated as if you yourselves were suffering.
>
> Marriage should be honored by all, and the marriage bed kept pure, for God will judge the adulterer and all the sexually immoral. Keep your lives free from the love of money and be content with what you have, because God has said,
>
> "Never will I leave you; never will I forsake you."
>
> So we say with confidence, "The Lord is my helper; I will not be afraid. What can human beings do to me?"

> Remember your leaders, who spoke the word of God to you. Consider the outcome of their way of life and imitate their faith. Jesus Christ is the same yesterday and today and forever.
>
> Do not be carried away by all kinds of strange teachings. It is good for our hearts to be strengthened by grace, not by the eating of ceremonial foods, which is of no benefit to those who observe such rituals. We have an altar from which those who minister at the tabernacle have no right to eat."[1]

Adam finished the entire chapter and said a few silent words before closing the book and putting it on the table beside the bed. When he got up he laid his hand on the book as if saying one final prayer before climbing into bed. He turned the lamp off, pulled the towel out from under the covers, dropped it on the floor and rolled over to go to sleep.

Again tonight he was dreaming about the beautiful woman. They walked hand in hand in the park. Adam saw himself in the dream looking at her lovingly, caressing her face and stroking her long blonde hair. They must be lovers. Tonight her hand came to his face and pushed his hair off his brow. He leaned down and gently kissed her. She leaned against his chest as he held her tight.

Adam woke up with a start. His heart was racing and he was sweating. He didn't understand why he kept having this same dream over and over. He ran his hand through his hair before getting out of bed to get a drink.

"Damn, who is she?" He said to himself leaning on the kitchen counter. "What does this mean? I don't know anyone like her."

Adam went back to bed but he had a very restless night and slept very little the rest of the night.

---

[1] **Hebrews 13: 1-10 The Bible: Today's New International Version**

Chapter 4

Adam was dressed and just about ready to grab a cupcake and some milk when there was a knock at his door. He figured it had to be Sally or Vic since they were the only two that could get to the top of the steps without the key. He opened the door to see Vic standing there with a smile on his face.

"You're up kinda early," Adam said to the youth who was ready to leave for school.

"You ready to go yet?" Vic simply asked Adam.

"I was just going to have a cupcake and some milk," Adam said turning toward the kitchen table. "You want one?"

"No," Vic said pulling on Adam's sleeve. "You have to eat breakfast at school with me."

"Oh yeah?" Adam seemed surprised. "That sounds better than cupcakes and milk. But I'm broke."

"Don't need money," Vic said pulling on Adam's sleeve. "Come on."

"Let me put the milk away and I'll be ready," Adam said.

"Where's your coat?" Vic asked looking around the room. "It's cold outside."

"I don't have one. I have to buy one yet," Adam said. "I won't freeze. Let's hurry."

When Adam stepped outside, the chill cut through him like a hunting knife. They could see their breath in the morning sunlight. Adam started walking faster to get over to school, but noticed that Vic limped a little. Oh, how he wanted to get in the warmth of the school cafeteria, but he didn't want to leave his little buddy behind.

Adam looked over to see how Vic was doing when his eyes caught the early morning sun shining through the trees with the Congregational Church steeple spiraling straight through the middle of the sun. Adam stopped and just looked at the wonder of it. He thanked the Lord for beautiful moments like this.

"What you waiting for?" Vic called back to Adam now almost an entire block ahead of him. Adam turned around to see Vic and was going to start jogging to catch up to him but wanted one more look at the sunrise. When he turned around, it was gone. God had given him that warm moment to let the young boy get ahead.

In the cafeteria, Adam was told he was to pay a minimal fee for breakfast which he didn't mind at all.

"Can't buy and cook food that cheap," Adam said as he took his tray over to sit next to Vic. At least Adam knew he would have a decent meal at a decent price twice a day for five days a week. And he would probably eat with Hal on the weekends. So he wouldn't have to worry too much about food. He could put most of his paycheck away to buy some kind of transportation for himself. But first, he would have to borrow Hal's car and go into Quincy to get some winter clothes.

On the way home from school that evening Adam noticed that it had warmed up quite a bit, but it was still cool. He jogged across the street and past the bank. He was heading towards his door when he heard his name being called. He turned around and looked but didn't see anyone. He heard the woman's voice the second time and homed in on the sound. It sounded like it was coming from the bank. He looked closer and he saw Sally standing near the back door of the bank. He jogged back to the bank to see what she had on her mind.

"I know Hal wanted you to come over for supper tonight," Sally started. "But, could you stop by the house before going. I have something I want to show you. Actually I have something for you."

"All right," Adam said. "If you don't mind, I'm going to head home to get warm. See you later."

"I'll be home in an hour," Sally called after him. He waved in acknowledgement as he ran across the lawns of the bank and her house.

Adam knocked on the back door of Sally's house on his way over to Hal's for supper. Vic opened the door and grabbed his sleeve to bring him into the house.

"I'm glad to see you, too, buddy," Adam said trying to make Vic let go of his sleeve.

"Victor, let him go," Sally scolded the young boy. "I'm sorry. He got so excited when I told him."

"You gonna like it," Vic said smiling from ear to ear shaking his fists.

"Adam, I told you that I lost my husband a while back," Sally said. Adam nodded. Vic bounced up and down with excitement. "Well, I never got rid of his clothes. There are some very nice jackets and things. When I saw you and Vic running this morning, I knew you had to be freezing. Come look at them and if they fit, you are more than welcome to anything."

"Sally, I," Adam started.

"Don't say anything. I just never thought about getting rid of the stuff." Sally explained that she and her husband were not married all that long and the only reason he married her was because of Vic. And when they found out that Vic was a "special" child, he couldn't handle it and joined the Army. He was gone more than he was home. "You look about his same size. I'd rather you have it than sending it to some thrift shop."

"Come look at it," Vic said pulling on Adam's sleeve again. "Come on." Adam gave in.

He let Vic lead him into a back bedroom where Sally had pulled some of the clothes out of a closet and laid them on the bed. Adam picked up a nice fleece lined jean jacket. He held it up and it looked like it would fit. When he tried it on, it felt as if it was custom made for him. Adam smiled. Vic clapped his hands. Sally smiled, too.

"Looks very nice on you," she said admiring him in the jacket.

"This is awfully nice of you, but this was an expensive jacket," Adam said taking the coat off and laying it on the bed.

"I didn't pay for it," Sally said. "There are also suits in here, jeans, dress slacks, shoes. If you need anything to wear, you can have it. There's even some of his old hunting clothes."

"Will you take me hunting some time?" Vic asked Adam with excitement all over his face.

"Buddy, I've never been hunting in my life," Adam said. "My dad was a forest ranger and he didn't believe in hunting. Only hunting we ever did was with a camera." Vic's face fell a bit but he understood.

"You better get over to Hal's," Sally said. "I'll have Vic take this upstairs for you."

"I don't want to take all of it from you," Adam said not wanting to be greedy. "Let me pay you something for it."

"You can shovel snow for it this winter," Sally said knowing very well that she has someone come with a blade to clear her drive when it snows.

"That's a deal," Adam said shaking her hand. Sally simply smiled.

"Nice jacket," Hal said when he opened the door to let Adam in. "Looks like it'd be a warm one."

"It is," Adam said looking at Hal when he took it off then hanging it on the back of the kitchen chair. "Did you know she was going to do that?"

"I might a put a bug in her ear," Hal said handing Adam a couple empty plates with silverware and napkins. "I knew you couldn't a had too much in that little bag a yours."

"Well, thanks," Adam said. "I really appreciate it. I really appreciate this jacket now that it's getting cold." Adam took a bowl of vegetables from Hal that he had just pulled from the oven and set them on the table.

"Cold! You think this is cold?" Hal laughed at Adam as he pulled out the roaster and handed it to the younger man. "This is just the beginning of fall. We ain't even had a frost yet." Hal pulled out a pan of biscuits and sat them on the table before taking his seat.

"Did you cook a whole other meal?" Adam said as he looked at the table from his seat.

"No, this is what we didn't eat last night," Hal said. "I do confess I made fresh biscuits though. I don't like left over biscuits. Dig in."

Adam lowered his head for a few seconds before taking anything off of the plate. Hal looked at the kid and thought maybe he had the right idea.

"You got any words to that prayer?" Hal asked. Adam looked up at Hal who was looking at him.

"Basically just thanking the Lord for the good food and good friends," Adam said.

"Amen," Hal said as he picked up the bowl of carrots and passed it to Adam with a wide smile.

After dinner while Adam helped Hal clean up the dishes Hal asked the young man how he liked his new job, his apartment and the town. Adam told him the apartment was great. It was all he needed; and the fact that it was close to his job was super since he didn't have a car.

Hal reminded him that if he ever needed to go into Quincy, he could always use the Taurus. Adam said his job was fine. He said it was honest money for honest work. The kids didn't give him a bad time like he thought they might. He said that he wondered if they are thinking he is going to be celebrity once race season starts. He couldn't believe that people knew who he was the first night he was in town.

"Hell, boy," Hal laughed. "You can't fart in this town without someone knowing about it." Adam didn't like that. He grew up in a small town and knew how the truth could get turned around so easily. "It's a joke, Adam," Hal said, patting him on the back.

"You know, Hal," Adam said. "It may be a joke, but the sad thing is, it's the truth." Hal's smile disappeared. He knew Adam was right. "You watch, by the end of the winter, they'll be talking that I'm sleeping with Sally. And that will be so far from the truth."

"What's wrong with Sally?" Hal asked wondering if Adam wasn't into women.

"Not a thing," Adam said. "She's a most desirable woman. But if I am going to be driving, I'm not going to get involved with any woman. My lover is going to have to be that car."

"Hey, that's what I like to hear," Hal said with a big grin. "I wish I had something to toast to you with. You're going to be like my son-in-law."

"You got some cocoa?" Adam said smiling, since he wanted something to warm him up before heading out into the cool night air.

Hal laughed as he walked to the stove to heat up some water. He got out a box of instant cocoa and took out some envelopes for their cocoa then threw the box in front of Adam.

"Take the rest of these home with you," Hal said with a smile. "Can't have my celebrity getting cold during these cold autumn nights."

As soon as the tea kettle whistled, Hal poured hot water in each cup over the cocoa mix. The smell, alone, helped to warm Adam's soul. It brought back memories of his mom's kitchen.

"Now, if we had some cookies, we'd be all set," Adam said. All of a sudden a bag of Chips Ahoy slid right in front of him. "Wow, I like it here. All I have to do is wish and it happens." Adam smiled as he opened the bag of cookies, took out a couple and slid the bag over to Hal.

“You knew I had them,” the old man said. “You did my shopping.” Hal took a cookie, dunked it in his cocoa and popped the whole thing in his mouth.

Hal not only gave Adam the cocoa, but sent him home with the rest of the roast, carrots and potatoes, a loaf of bread, a stick of butter, and a bag of groceries that would hold him over until the weekend. Hal knew that Adam was getting paid on Friday and Hal was planning to ask Adam to take him to the grocery store on Saturday. At least the kid wouldn’t have to shop at the Quick Stop.

Chapter 5

Adam was pretty happy with his first paycheck from school. After Sally cashed his check he paid her rent, opened a savings account and still had plenty to go shopping with. He and Hal had plans to go into Quincy on Saturday morning to get Hal's groceries.

"So kid, what do you think of it so far?" Hal asked Adam on the way into town.

"Think of what?" Adam asked as he pulled onto the by-pass.

"This…the town, the people, your job," Hal explained.

"Oh, I like everything just fine," Adam said smiling. "It'll be a lot better once we start racing. To be real honest it's kind of boring around town and I imagine it'll get worse once winter sets in."

"That'll be a fact," Hal said nodding his head. "We play a lot a cards, checkers and dominoes. And then there's the TV."

"My folks would like this town," Adam said recalling his small town of Bevier.

"They small town people, are they?" Hal looked over to Adam noticing the kid was far away in thought.

"Yeah," Adam said softly. "I miss them, too."

"How long's it been since you been home to see 'em?" Hal wondered if there had been some kind of a fuss between the boy and his family.

"It's been about six months I guess," Adam said. "I haven't talked to my momma since I started work here. I really should call." Adam wasn't really talking to Hal, but more so to himself.

"How far of a drive is it?" Hal wanted to know.

"From here," Adam was figuring it up in his mind. "I guess it is about an hour and a half or so."

"That ain't so far," Hal said. "Shame on you, not going home more often."

"Well, it's kind of hard since I don't have a car," Adam said stating the obvious.

"Call your momma and tell her to expect us for supper," Hal said as he handed Adam his phone when they were walking into Wal-mart.

"You serious?" Adam asked taking the phone from Hal. The old man nodded with a smile.

"Sure," he grinned. "I'd like to meet the folks that raised such a fine young man."

After putting away their groceries, Adam and Hal headed west through Hannibal on Missouri Highway 36 to the small town of Bevier. Once they went through Macon and pass Long Branch State Park, Adam knew it was a matter of minutes before he would be home again. After turning off the highway and onto N. Macon Street, Adam went just a few blocks into town and pulled into the driveway on the right hand side of the street of a large pink house with gray shutters. Hal knew that home looked as though it had seen a large family, with the big porch on the front and the flag waving in the front yard. A pretty brown haired girl came out onto the porch when the car pulled into the drive way. When she saw it was Adam, she ran to the car.

"Adam," she cried running into his arms as he picked her up swinging her around. Hal got out of the car and walked over to them.

"Ava, this is my boss, Hal Graves," Adam introduced his youngest sister to his boss.

"Glad to meet you, Mr. Graves," Ava said as she extended her hand. Hal shook the girl's hand.

"You, too, missy," Hal said. Then to Adam he said, "She's a lot prettier than you." Adam smiled seeing the compliment made Ava blush.

"Come on in the house. Momma fixed a nice supper just for you," Ava said pulling on Adam's arm. "I hope you like trout," she said to Hal. "Daddy brought some home yesterday and it's way too much just for us. And you know how Momma hates to freeze good fish."

Lydia Dieker was so happy to see her son. She dropped what she was doing and immediately gave him a hug as if she hadn't seen him for years. Lydia was a very pretty woman who looked much younger than her 53 years. Adam had his mother's soft, sensitive eyes and shiny light brown hair which she wore in a short curled bob pulled to one side with a small barrette.

Dan Dieker walked in the back door with the same greeting for his son. Dan was a tall and strong man, thick through the shoulders and narrow at the waist. Dan was a very handsome man. He and Adam shared the same strong jaw line and chin. Dan's smile lit up the room just as Adam's does. When Dan extended his hand to shake Hal's hand, Hal noticed how big it was. Hal could tell Dan was a working man. Hal liked Adam's family. He understood now how Adam was such a good man.

After dinner Hal leaned back in his chair and patted his belly. When Ava asked him if he wanted anything else, Hal could only shake his head.

"Would you like some coffee?" Lydia asked him holding up a cup.

"That I will take, thanks," Hal said sitting straight up again.

Lydia poured Hal a cup of coffee as Adam got the milk and passed it to him.

"I bet this old house could tell some stories," Hal said to Adam as he took a sip of coffee.

"More than you know," Adam said grinning.

"This house belonged to my father," Lydia said. "My mother passed away just before Dan and I were married and my dad asked if we wanted to live with him until we found something for ourselves. As you can see, we never found anything better. Before we knew it, I was pregnant and Alice came along. A couple years later we had Angela and it seems the next time I looked we had all seven of them."

"Did I notice a trend in names," Hal said. "Alice, Angela, Adam and Ava…tell me the other names begin with A, too."

"You're right," Lydia laughed. "It wasn't really planned that way until Adam came along. We just really like the names. Then when Andrew came along, we couldn't change then."

"So what are the others," Hal asked with anticipation.

"Alice, Angela, Adele, Adam, Andrew, Aaron and me," Ava said proudly.

"Sounds like a mighty fine family," Hal said. Ava handed him the latest family picture taken at Angela's wedding two years ago. "Very nice looking family, too. Adam you look like your brothers."

"Yeah, we all look a lot alike," Adam said. "I think the Dieker gene is pretty strong because we all look like our cousins, too." Ava laughed.

"So do you think he'll make you proud over there?" Dan asked Hal referring to the racing.

"I'm sure he will," Hal said pulling out his phone. "Here is a picture of our baby we're gonna be working on." Hal handed Dan his phone showing him a picture of the black beauty. Hal reached over and pushed a button on the phone to get to the next picture.

"What a beauty," Dan said passing the phone to Lydia with Ava looking over her shoulder. "Have you taken it out yet, son?"

"No, Dad, not yet," Adam said. "We won't start until after the holidays."

"So how do you like your job over there?" Dan asked somewhat disappointed Adam didn't stay and work with him until race season started again.

"I like it. It's honest pay for honest work," Adam repeated a quote that he had heard over and over during his life from both his grandfather and his dad. Dan nodded getting up to refill his cup of coffee, offering a refill to Hal.

Adam got up from the kitchen table and walked into the living room. He stood at the front window looking across the road toward the old church on the corner and down Livingston Street. He wasn't looking at anything in particular but just letting his mind drift back to the days when he and his brothers played ball until dark or rode their bikes down old highway 36 to the park to go fishing.

"What are you thinking about?" Ava asked her older brother as she walked up putting her arm around him and leaning her head against his shoulder. Adam leaned his head against hers.

"A simpler time, I guess," he said slipping his arm around her. "I'm thinking about the fun we had when we were kids when everyone was home. I'm remembering about a time when we played outside all day, not having to worry about anything except who was going to get the biggest piece of whatever dessert Mom made for supper."

"So how's school going?" Adam wanted to come back to the present and push the past back where it belongs.

"This year's a beast," Ava said as she walked away from Adam. "I'm trying to get all my gen ed finished this semester so I can start on my major classes. I have got a bear of a schedule."

"You still have your mind set on double majoring in Pre-law and History at Truman?" Adam asked her. Ava nodded. "Isn't that going to be pretty tough?"

"Yeah, it is. But I want to go to SLU for my law degree so I have to work hard and get good grades," Ava said. "I really want to do well so I can get part of that paid for."

"Well, you know I'll help you anyway I can," Adam said. "With this car Hal has, it may be a winner. I've got a backer now and will be able to hit some high paying tracks. So, what I get, I'll see to it you get your college paid for."

"Adam, I appreciate it," Ava said. "But, if you don't win all of your races, I'll understand. I'll still love just for offering." Ava gave Adam a big hug then the two of them walked back into the kitchen.

"I enjoyed visiting with your parents," Hal said as they were heading toward Illinois.

"Yeah, I bet," Adam said. "Mom probably told you a bunch of stories about me when I was little. And Dad told you what to do with me when I fly off the handle." Adam laughed.

"No, neither of those," Hal said looking over at Adam. "They did tell me about some things that happened in your family they thought I should know about to understand you."

"Oh yea," Adam said as his smile disappeared. "And what might that have been?"

"Your dad told me about some people you kids looked up to that more or less turned on you," Hal said seeing Adam was getting upset just at the thought.

"He shouldn't have said anything," Adam said. Then after a few seconds he said, "More or less? He said they more or less turned on us. Or were those your words?" Adam was very upset.

"I'm sorry boy. I shouldn't have said anything," Hal apologized.

"So did he go into details?" Adam briefly looked over to Hal who had his head down.

"Not really," Hal said. "But, he mentioned a little something."

"I'll tell you the way it was then," Adam said. "My dad always sugar coats it." Adam began the story of when he was a child.

As Lydia had told Hal, she and Dan moved in with her father after they had married. Her mother had died from a long battle with cancer a few years earlier and Lydia actually felt she needed to stay with her dad to take care of him. Dan had his good job and figured he could save money for later. But, the children came and the family stayed with Grandpa Rees. The house was big enough until the fourth baby was born. The first three girls were in one bedroom. Grandpa had his own room and Lydia and Dan had their room. When Adam came along, his crib was in his parents' room until Andrew came along. Adam then had to go sleep with Grandpa. By the time Aaron had to move in with them, they would throw a feather bed on the floor for the boys. But, being little tykes, they liked to sleep in the big bed with Grandpa.

The three little boys loved their grandfather and he paid special attention to them, playing ball with them, telling them stories and always having an extra quarter or dollar for them. One year, when Adam was about six, the boys got bunk beds for Grandpa's room. Adam had his own bed and the two younger boys shared the bottom bunk. The little ones still liked to climb into the big bed when it was cold to sleep with Grandpa. Adam thought they were sissies.

One night Adam heard Aaron softly crying below him. He looked under and asked him what was wrong. Grandpa wouldn't let Aaron sleep in the big bed that night. Adam told him not to be a baby and go to sleep. Adam was almost asleep when he heard someone whimpering but this time it sounded like it was coming from Grandpa's bed. Adam looked over and from the light of the street light he could see Grandpa's head over Andrew's belly. Andrew's little hands were trying to push the big man's head away. Adam watched for a minute or two until the grandfather pulled his head away exposing the naked little boy. The grandfather put his arm around the boy and whispered in his ear how much he loved him and that they had a special secret. Through his tears Andrew nodded.

As Andrew was pulling on his shorts and jumping out of the big bed to go to his bed, Grandpa saw Adam watching him. They stared at each other for what seemed a long time before the grandfather rolled over to go to sleep.

When Adam asked Andrew about what had happened, Andrew denied anything. Aaron looked at Andrew begging him with his eyes to let Adam in on the secret. Every time Adam saw the grandfather, the old man stared at him and even threatened him. So Adam never told. But none of the boys said anything and the abuse went on until the grandfather passed away four years later. Adam was so angry with his brothers that to this day, there is somewhat of a rift between them because of it. His older sisters blamed him for not telling and he is not as close to them as he would like either.

"I'm so sorry, son," Hal said. "Your dad didn't go into details. He just said you never let anyone get close to you and it takes you a long time to gain someone's trust."

"He's partly right about that," Adam said. "It does take a while for me to totally trust someone, but I am not planning to get like engaged close any time soon. But, I would like to think you and I are kind of close."

"I'd like to think that, too," Hal said. "And son, I'll never intentionally hurt you. You have my word on that."

"Thanks Hal," Adam said. "You have mine, too."

Chapter 6

Adam had brought back Ava's old laptop with him and in the evenings he researched the tracks where he would be racing next summer. Some of the tracks he had been on before and knew them quite well while others would be new to him. Most of them were quarter mile tracks in the Tri-state area but there were a few that were far away. Adam didn't care to drive a long distance before racing, or going to a race venue where the team would have to spend the night. But he was not making the calls and would go where ever Hal wanted to race the car.

Since he had the laptop Adam and Ava kept in contact almost daily. She would fill him in on family stuff, letting him know that he was sorely missed and tried desperately to talk him into coming home for Thanksgiving. He would write back to her about his job, the kids, Hal and the friends he was making and not mention the holiday.

"You going home for Thanksgiving." Hal mentioned the holiday on the Monday of the week before.

"I thought I'd stay here and see if you were cooking," Adam said half joking.

"You should go home," Hal told the young man. "Mend some bridges."

"Don't go there, Hal," Adam said getting up to rinse off his plate from supper.

"But, Adam…" Hal was cut short.

"They're not my bridges to mend," Adam said. "They know the facts. They can come to me now. I tried enough times to mend your so called bridges." Adam was visibly upset. "Thanks for supper," he said as he walked out the front door and down the street to his place.

"Adam, I sure am glad you're staying with us today," Vic said when Adam walked in to the house below his apartment.

"Me, too, buddy," Adam said handing Vic an apple pie. "What smells so good in here?" Adam asked as he walked into the kitchen seeing Hal there rolling out homemade rolls and putting them on the cookie sheet.

"Well, it's not homemade apple pie," Sally teased him taking the pie from Vic.

"It was homemade at the grocery store," Adam said. "That place smelled just as good as your kitchen when I picked it up." Adam teased. "Can I help you with anything?"

"No, we just have to wait for the turkey to get done." Sally looked around. "The potatoes are ready to cook, the beans are ready to put into the oven, and the sweet potatoes are in the oven now," she kept thinking aloud. "My folks should be here in an hour or so, and my sister Donna should be here anytime."

"There she is now," Vic called when he heard the doorbell ring. He ran to the door to allow Donna and her new boyfriend in the house.

After introductions, Donna went in to the kitchen to see what she could do to help Sally. Her boyfriend, Jeff Hansen stayed in the living room with Vic and Adam and immediately started talking about racing.

"I saw you up in Lee County a couple years ago," Jeff said. "You slid across that finish line leaving the rest of the field so far behind," Jeff said smiling and remembering the race.

"That was a fun one," Adam said remembering the sweet victory.

"You didn't do much after that," Jeff said. "At least your name dropped off the rosters."

"Yea," Adam said. "I got hurt and couldn't finish the season and was out all year last year."

"I bet you were bumming about that," Jeff said. Adam nodded. "What happened?"

"I broke my knee and had to have surgery," Adam said remembering the incident. "It just took a very long time to heal."

"So do you think Hal's car has a chance?" Jeff asked Adam but young Vic jumped in.

"You bet she does. It's gonna be a sweet ride, huh, Adam?" Vic got so excited when he talked about the car and racing.

"Well, I haven't taken it out yet," Adam said. "But she sure is pretty."

"I heard it before. And it sounds like a monster," Vic said patting

Adam on the arm. "You'll be able to handle her."

Sally's parents arrived then and just that quickly Vic forgot about racing and ran to see his grandparents. Adam smiled at him but Jeff laughed at the youngster.

"He'd drive me crazy," Jeff said. "He's up and down like a yo-yo like that all the time. Doesn't he get in your way while you're working and stuff?"

"Not at all," Adam said. "Vic's a good kid. He knows more about racing than most of the drivers. I've been listening and learning a lot from him." Adam got up and walked over to meet Sally's parents.

"This is my grandpa and grandma," Vic said introducing Adam to his grandparents. Adam was happy to meet them. Jeff walked over extending his hand to Ben and Julie Wavering.

"Glad to see you again," Ben said to Jeff but Julie just walked into the kitchen to be with the women after she met Adam.

"He's very handsome," Julie said to Sally as she put a basket of food on the table.

"It's not like that, Mom," Sally said to her mother. "He's here to race and that is his only interest at the moment. Ask Victor who Adam's girlfriend is. It is so cute."

"So he and Vic get along real well?" Julie asked her daughter looking into the living room, seeing Vic practically sitting on Adam's lap talking about racing.

"He and Adam hit it off from day one," Sally said. "I've never seen him so attached."

"But there's nothing between the two of you?" Donna asked. Sally shook her head. "Would you like there to be?"

"I don't know," Sally said looking at the very handsome young man. "I really don't know. I think I am happy just being friends."

"Have you slept with him yet?" Donna asked straight out.

"Donna!" Sally and her mother both cried out at the same time.

The men looked into the kitchen at the outburst but went right back to their conversation when they saw nothing was wrong.

"Donna that is none of your business," Julie scolded her daughter.

"That's OK Mom," Sally said. "I'm not like her." Sally dug at her sister. "No, we haven't and I don't plan to." Sally got up and put the potatoes on the stove and the green beans in the oven.

"I think it's a shame," Julie said. "He's such a nice guy. And he's so good with Vic."

"Mom," Sally said as she passed her stopping at the kitchen door. "Dad, will you carve the turkey for me, please?" Turning around, Sally shook her finger at her mom and sister as a warning to change the subject in front of her father when he came in the kitchen.

Sally set up a buffet of sorts in the kitchen and let people fill their plates before finding a seat in the dining room. The table was extended to its fullest and everyone just fit around it. The small dining room was very cozy during the meal. Vic was the delegated runner if someone wanted seconds, but after the third request he started bringing in the platter of turkey, the bowl of mashed potatoes, and other big bowls. No one left the table hungry and none of the pies were touched right away.

Sally and Julie thanked Vic and Adam and took the dishes from them when they tried to help the ladies clear the table, and ushered them into the living room with the other men. Jeff had turned on the football game and he and Ben were discussing the valors of the Dallas Cowboys.

"So what do you think of the Cowboys, Adam?" Jeff asked when Adam and Vic walked in and sat down on the sofa.

"To be real honest, I like the cheerleaders," Adam said with a smile which cracked up Vic. He elbowed Adam and rolled off the sofa laughing. Ben had to laugh at that joke and even Jeff thought it was a bit cute.

"So, you're not into football?" Jeff asked. Adam shook his head.

"I'd rather watch a high school team in any sport," Adam said. "But when they get paid millions to play a game, that's when I lose interest."

"What about you? Don't you get paid big bucks for what you do?" Jeff asked. Adam smiled.

"Do you think if I made that much money I'd be living in a small apartment in Payson, working as a janitor in a school and borrowing a car when I want to go somewhere?" Adam sent the question back.

"Well, you haven't raced yet," Jeff reminded Adam.

"I ran the circuit for five years before I got hurt," Adam reminded Jeff.

"Oh yeah, that's right," Jeff said. "And you were pretty high up every year in points. That last year you might have won it, too." Jeff paused for a moment. "So you don't make big bucks racing?"

"Not unless you are on the big circuit or your name is Earnhardt or Gordon. I'm not that good, yet," Adam said humbly.

"Once you get in the black beauty you will be," Vic said banging on Adam's arm.

"Let's hope so," Adam said. "Let's hope Hal gets a crew that can get her up to snuff."

"Got a very good team lined up for spring," Hal said. "And I got somebody coming up from Daytona to check her out after the holidays. No promises yet from him, though."

"What are the chances of seeing this black beauty today?" Jeff asked.

"I suppose we could walk up there if you want," Hal said. "We could walk off a little of that good supper." Then teasing Adam he said, "We could make room for some of that homemade apple pie."

The entire family took a walk up the street to take a look at the car. Vic trotted ahead since Hal had given him the key and he had the doors open and lights on in the garage. Without the sunlight bouncing off the chrome and the shiny black car, it just didn't look as exciting as it did the first time Adam saw it. But it was still a magnificent piece of machinery.

"She sure is a beauty," Ben said walking around the car being careful not to touch her afraid of leaving finger prints.

"Can't say much for the interior," Julie joked looking in the window.

"Grandma, they don't have seats except for Adam," Vic explained to his grandmother. She hugged her grandson explaining she was teasing and Vic laughed at her.

"So Hal, how does someone go about sponsoring a car like this?" Ben asked walking over toward the older man wanting to talk about using his lawn care business as a sponsor.

"You serious?" Hal was delighted Ben would even suggest such a thing. "Let's you and me talk after the holiday." Ben extended his hand to Hal and nodded his head.

While the family was still standing around and talking about the car, Julie walked over to Adam and Vic.

"Adam, I was told that you don't have a girlfriend, yet," Julie said more as a joke knowing he wasn't looking. Vic pulled on his grandmother's sleeve.

"Yes, he does, grandma," Vic said then looking up at Adam.

"You do?" Julie asked playing along with Vic. "Well, who is she?"

"A black beauty 350 stock car," Adam and Vic said together and they both pointed toward the car. Vic started laughing so hard. It tickled Julie, and Adam started laughing knowing something so simple made the boy happy.

Chapter 7

"You've got to make an appearance over the holidays," Ava begged Adam.

"Why? So I can sit and listen to all the crap I get every time the whole family is together," Adam reminded his sister. "I don't think so, Ava. I'm pretty happy right here."

"Mom's going to be pretty sad." Ava was laying on the guilt trip.

"When she starts sticking up for me, I'll think about coming home," Adam said. "I never should've let that old man talk me into taking him over there in the first place."

"I'll miss you," Ava said very sad she didn't talk him into coming home.

"I'll miss you, too. I wish things weren't the way they are," Adam said before ending the call to the only person he keeps in contact with in his family. Maybe he would try to get together with just her over the break. That is, if his parents would allow their nineteen-year old daughter to drive alone to see him.

Adam needed to get his mind on something else. He wished they would start working on the car, but Hal wasn't planning on doing anything until mid January. That was still a month away. Winter had just started, the holiday season always got him down, there was nothing to do and he was going stir crazy. There were only so many movies one could watch, so many games of checkers one could play and only so much surfing the web one could do. He needed a road trip. But where would he go?

"Hal, what do you do for Christmas?" Adam asked one evening after supper.

"I usually just have dinner with Sally and her family. Then I come home. Why you ask?" Hal replied.

"I've been so bored around here lately I thought about taking a road trip," Adam said.

"Sounds interesting," Hal said. "Where you going?"

"I was thinking of going to England," Adam said as he watched the expression on the old man's face change from interest to excitement.

"England," Hal exclaimed. "Why on earth you want to go all the way over there?"

"It's the closest place I could find having races at this time of year," Adam explained. "I was thinking of leaving either Christmas day or the day after. They have their last two BriSCA Formula One at Belle Vue on the 27th and Kings Lynn on the 28th. I thought it would be kind of fun to go. You want to go with me?"

"That'll cost quite a bit," Hal said.

"I don't have anything else to spend my money on," Adam countered.

"True," Hal was breaking down. "You got a passport?" Adam nodded.

"Had to get one last year when I went to Canada," he replied running his hand through his hair. "I really wish we could take Vic along. He'd get a thrill out of going. You think Sally would let him?"

"You don't want to drag that boy across the globe with you," Hal argued. Then thinking, he said, "Not unless you want to take his mama, too."

"What do you mean by that?" Adam asked not liking the tone Hal used.

"Just saying it would be a nice trip for Sally, too," Hal said with a smile.

"That's not what you meant, you old goat," Adam said getting up from the table.

"Come back here, kid," Hal ordered. "Sit down! That's probably why you're bored. You need a woman in your life."

"Don't start with me, Hal," Adam said as he sat back down at the table.

"Ain't you interested in women?" Hal asked straight out.

"Not at the moment," Adam replied not getting the gist of Hal's question.

"I mean, son, you do like girls, don't you?" Hal asked again rearranging the words. Adam caught on this time.

"For Christ's sake, Hal. Sure I like women," Adam cried. "Doesn't mean I have to have one all the time. There are some men that use their brains to think with instead of their…"

"OK, OK, I'm sorry," Hal said. "It's just that there are some awful pretty girls chasing you and you haven't even noticed. A guy has to wonder."

"Yeah, I've noticed," Adam said running his hand through his hair. "And if I didn't have a big racing season coming up, I'd sure take 'em up on it,"

"You could still go out with them and have a little fun now and then," Hal said. Adam shook his head.

"That's not who I am, Hal," Adam said.

"No, it's not," Hal said looking over at the good looking young man.

"I'm sure he'd love to go," Sally said when Adam asked if Vic could go to England with him after Christmas. "I just don't know if I want him to go that far without me."

"You can come along, too," Adam said which took Sally totally by surprise.

"Oh, Adam, I don't know," Sally said thinking how wonderful such a trip would be for both of them. "I do have some vacation time coming. I'd have to find our passports. Oh, I don't know." Sally was just mumbling to herself more than to Adam.

"Is it a matter of paying for it?" Adam asked her.

"No, that's not a problem," Sally said. "I've been putting money in our rainy day account for quite some time and this could be a good time to use it."

"Then, what's holding you back?" Adam didn't understand what the problem was.

"You said Hal is going, too?" Sally asked looking into Adam's eyes.

"Yeah, he's going," Adam answered her. "You know Vic would get a bang out of going."

"Well, to be quite honest, that is why I am hesitating," Sally said. "You know how Vic is around here. He's all happy and pretty much knows where he is and what he's doing. But when he's in a strange place; well, he gets nervous. He actually gets frightened and acts out. When we went up to Canada last spring on the train, he was so antsy that I needed to give him medication to calm him down. He was so hard for me to handle. I am almost afraid to say yes."

"You'll have Hal and me this time to help," Adam said. "And we can get medication for him if need be. I think that if he is with us and we keep him interested in where we are going and what we are going to do, he won't worry about the people. I really think it would be worth the try."

"Adam, last time I had to make him wear diapers," Sally said lowering her head to hide a tear. "He couldn't help himself."

"We can plan ahead for that, too," Adam said. "I'm willing to work with him, if you are. And I am sure Hal will be, too. And look, if he can handle going on this trip, he'll be able to go to the races with us next year."

"What do you mean; go to the races with you?" Sally asked wrinkling her forehead.

"He's going to be a part of my pit crew. I thought you knew," Adam said. "So, he'll be going with us to all the races. And you won't be with him all the time."

"I most certainly will be," Sally corrected Adam.

"I don't think so," Adam reminded Sally. "Women aren't allowed in the pits."

After much more discussion, it was finally decided that Sally and Vic would take the trip with Adam and Hal. Now was the time to tell Vic.

Adam was sitting at Sally's kitchen table with the laptop when Vic came in. Adam had the BriSCA Formula One Stock Car page open and was looking at some of the cars.

"Wow, those look pretty cool," Vic said as he leaned over Adam's shoulder. "I never seen them race before."

"How would you like to go watch these guys?" Adam asked Vic.

"For real?" Vic asked.

"For real," Adam said as he flipped the page to some of the drivers' pictures.

"I don't recognize any of these guys," Vic said looking at the pictures.

"That's because they don't drive in America," Adam said. "They drive in a country called England…way across the Atlantic Ocean." Vic's eyes were huge.

"We studied that in school," Vic said. "That's where Big Ben is."

"Right," Adam said amazed that the youngster knew about Big Ben and England. "Would you like to go over there and watch them race these cars?"

"Won't it be at the same time when you're racing?" Vic asked.

"Nope," Adam replied. "As a matter of fact they are racing right now."

"In the winter time?" Vic couldn't believe it.

"It's not winter where they are. They are still racing until the first of the year," Adam explained. "How would you like to go the day after Christmas?"

Vic looked at Adam, then he looked at his mom. Sally nodded her head. Vic let out a war hoop that could be heard down at Hal's house.

"I take it that's a yes," Adam asked.

"You darn tooting," Vic answered as he grabbed Adam and hugged him before going over to hug his mom. "You going, too, Mom?"

"I'm going, too, honey," Sally said at which Vic hugged his mom again. "And Victor, Hal's going, too."

"Oh my gosh, we're all going," Vic said slapping his forehead. "This is the best thing that has ever happened to me." Adam couldn't believe how making the boy happy made himself feel so good. He was just as excited now about the trip as Vic was.

The big day finally arrived. The tickets were from Quincy to Chicago to London. Sally was so nervous at how everything would affect Vic that she was getting upset.

"Calm down, girl, or you'll make yourself sick," Hal warned her. "Vic is doing just fine. Adam will keep an eye on him." Sally nodded knowing the old man was right.

They went through security at the small regional airport with no problems. Vic was so excited to go for his first airplane ride. They had told Vic that the plane from Quincy to Chicago was going to be small and kind of noisy so he would know what to expect, but he was still excited. When they walked out on to the tarmac to get on the plane, Vic grabbed Adam's hand. Adam was worried Vic was getting scared.

"Adam," Vic yelled over the sound of the plane.

"What is it, buddy?" Adam leaned down to the lad.

"Can I sit by you on the plane?" Vic asked calmly with a smile on his face.

"Sure, buddy, no problem," Adam said as he put his arm around

Vic's shoulders.

When they got on the plane Vic sat next to the window and Adam helped him with the seatbelt before sitting down next to him. Hal and Sally sat in front of them. There were only five other people on the small plane. When it began to taxi Adam explained what was happening to Vic. He was excited but listened carefully. When the plane went faster, Vic leaned over to Adam.

"I think we're going faster than most race cars," Vic yelled to Adam.

"I think so, too," Adam said as they both laughed.

When the plane lifted off the ground Vic's eyes became huge as platters. His mouth opened wide and he started laughing. Adam smiled at his excitement. Adam pointed out the window and Adam looked down pointing at different landmarks.

"There's Mill Creek," he hollered. "There's the raceway!"

"Sure enough," Adam said looking out the tiny port hole.

Vic stared out the window for the entire way to Chicago. When it was time to land, Adam had him sit back in his seat. He warned him that he would feel a little bump when the plane hit the ground so not to worry. Vic nodded and waited. The pilot landed the plane so smoothly that neither of them felt the wheels touch ground.

"You hang on to me," Adam ordered Vic once they were off the plane and heading for the terminal at O'Hare. Vic nodded and grabbed Adam's hand tightly. Adam could tell the boy was a little nervous since he had a death grip on his hand.

Once inside, a transporter met them with a wheel chair.

"Sir, would you like to have a seat?" The transporter asked Hal. He looked confused at her.

"Sir, we were called ahead and told you were going to Gate C23. That is quite a walk and your plane is leaving in three hours," she explained. "If I were you and had the opportunity, I'd take the chair. It's at least a forty-five minute walk."

Hal didn't hesitate and sat down. They no sooner started walking when Vic pulled Adam over to the side. He had to go to the bathroom.

"I'll be right back," Vic said as he let go of Adam's hand and walked toward the Men's Room. Adam quickly followed him. He didn't make a big scene about Vic letting go of his hand, but he sure didn't want the boy to go to the restroom in the airport by himself.

"Adam, do I still have to wear these things?" Vic asked him

referring to the diapers.

"Yeah, buddy, you do," Adam answered him. "We have a long way to go yet. Now we are going to get on a great big plane and you will probably sleep on it, too. It's best you leave them on." Adam talked to him while he was doing his thing.

"Will it be like all night?" Vic asked while he washed his hands.

"Almost," Adam said.

"What if we get hungry?" Vic asked when they were walking back to the others.

"They feed us. We'll probably get a couple meals," Adam said grabbing Vic's hand again as the group started walking.

Vic was so excited when he saw the big planes docked along each side of the concourse. Lisa, the transporter, told him that those were small planes compared to the one that he would be taking to England. His feet were gliding over the floor as he watched the planes take off and land as they continued their trek to their concourse.

Vic was disappointed when they had to get on an elevator and go down under the runways to cross over to a different section of the airport. But when he stepped out and saw the tunnel with its flashing neon and the people movers, his excitement returned fourfold. He stopped Adam at the beginning of the people mover a bit nervous as how to get on.

"It's just like stepping on an escalator," Adam said encouraging the boy.

Vic started walking and walked right on and almost fell into Adam. He didn't want to stand still, though. He saw other people walking by them and he wanted to walk, too. So, he and Adam started walking. Adam reminded him to keep walking when then came to the end and he did just that. When he was off of it, he was so happy. Then he saw another one ahead, he ran and got on right away.

"Vic, you wait for me," Adam ordered.

Vic kept walking around people, quite quickly, too. It was hard for Adam to catch up to him. Adam was getting tired by the time they had gotten to the third stretch. He knew the boy couldn't go anywhere, but he still worried. When he got to the end of the fourth stretch, there was a security guard with his hand on Vic's shoulder. Vic's head was down.

"Thank you," Adam said out of breath taking Vic by the hand and walking over to the side where they waited for Hal, Sally and Lisa.

"I'm sorry," Vic whispered almost too softly for Adam to hear.

"We won't say anything to the others if you promise you won't ever do that again," Adam said holding Vic's face in his hands. "Got it?" Vic nodded. "OK, over, done with, gone."

"Over, done with, gone," the boy repeated and gave Adam a hug.

The two of them sat along a ridge on the side of the long tunnel and had to wait almost ten minutes for the others to catch up with them.

"Where you been?" Vic asked them.

"Yeah, we just had a five course dinner waiting on you all," Adam said which made Vic break into laughter.

"Well, if I could take this chair on that thing, we'd be here with you enjoying that dinner," Lisa played along.

Once they got to their gate, everyone said good-bye to Lisa and thanked her for the help.

"We would never have found our way without her," Sally said. Hal and Adam agreed.

"We've still got an hour before boarding, anything you want to do?" Adam asked everyone.

"I'm hungry," Vic said looking around at the different places to eat.

"I brought you a snack," Sally said pulling a bag out of her carry-on. When she handed it to Vic, he pulled out an apple, a sandwich and a bottle of water.

"How'd you get that on with you?" Adam asked very surprised.

"No problem when you know people," she said winking at Adam.

"I'm serious," Adam said. "How'd you get that by security?"

"It was in my bag and I just put it on the scanner and it went through," Sally said.

"You don't have any more, do you?" Adam asked.

"No, I just knew that Vic would be hungry before we got on the plane to England so I brought something to hold him over," Sally said. "I'll be damned if I am going to pay these high prices for the same thing I can buy at home for a tenth of the price."

"Adam Dieker, please come to the ticket counter. Adam Dieker, to the ticket counter, please," said a voice over the loud speaker.

Adam looked up and couldn't imagine what was going on. Maybe something was wrong at home with his family. Too bad, he was not giving up this trip. He grabbed his ticket, boarding pass and passport and walked over to the ticket counter.

"I'm Adam Dieker," he said to the ticket agent.

"Sir, I was wondering if you would be willing to be upgraded to First Class," the agent said. "We have some last minute stand-bys that want tickets."

"Well, ma'am," Adam said as he pointed back toward the others. "I have three others with me."

"Splendid," the agent said. "That is just the number of seats I need. You'll make my job easier if you will take them all."

Adam motioned to Sally to get all the tickets, boarding passes and passports and come to the counter. After he told her the story, she was tickled they were being upgraded. The agent changed their tickets, and their boarding passes.

"Thank you, sir," the agent said. "Have a nice holiday."

When they told Hal what happened he was thrilled.

"This is a nicer airplane than the other one," Vic said when they were seated.

"You better believe it," Adam said when he snuggled in his big comfy first-class lounge chair. This was the first time he had ever been in first class and he had heard it was nice, but never like this. He even had room to stretch out his long legs.

"Pretty sweet, eh boy," Hal said to Adam from across the aisle.

"Very sweet," Adam said smiling. "I could get used to this."

Vic had his nose to the window when the plane roared down the runway. He watched as the buildings, cars and people became smaller and smaller. He saw the sun dancing on Lake Michigan as they were making their turn to head east and then gradually Chicago was so tiny he could no longer see it. Instead he saw snow covered farm lands, ribbons of high ways, and lots of wooded areas. Things were starting to get fuzzy and harder to see. Then below him everything was white and puffy. The sky was a glorious blue.

"Adam, everything disappeared," Vic said pointing out the window.

"Oh, it's still there," Adam said. "We're just high above the clouds right now."

"No way," Vic cried. "We're that high? Higher than the clouds? Are we in Heaven?"

"No, buddy, not quite that high," Adam laughed at him.

After a nice meal and a movie, Vic curled up to get some sleep.

Adam showed him how to put his seat back and he was pretty comfortable. The flight attendant asked him if he wanted a pillow and blanket. He smiled when she handed them to him and curled up with them. He was all set. Within minutes Vic was sound asleep.

"So far so good," Adam said to his two other traveling companions referring to the youngster.

"I was so worried how he would take to flying," Sally said. "I think we caught a break getting bumped to first class."

Chapter 8

When the plane landed in London, it was quite cloudy and cold. Adam had a car waiting for them and had asked for one with ONSTAR installed. Even though his order was filled he still asked the attendant how to get out of the airport to head toward Manchester. Once he had a map, directions and was confident they could find their way, he grabbed his bag and led the group out to the car.

"This is a funny looking car," Vic said as he threw his bag in the trunk with the others.

"I don't care what it looks like as long as it gets us there," Hal said. Adam agreed.

"Hey Adam, you're driving on the wrong side of the street," Vic tried to correct Adam.

"If you notice, Vic, everyone else is, too," Adam said giving the boy a chance to check things out. "Here in England, they drive on the left hand side of the road."

"That's weird," Vic said. "Do they race backwards, too?"

Adam thought a minute and then looked at Hal who shrugged his shoulders.

"I don't know, bud," Adam said. "I guess we'll find that out tomorrow."

"How long will it take to get to Manchester?" Sally asked before Vic.

"It's almost three and a half hours," Adam said. "I figured we could stop either at Stratford On Avon or Warwick and get a bite to eat for lunch."

"Stratford On Avon," Sally said thinking hard. "Isn't that the home of Shakespeare?"

"I think so," Adam said.

"Oh, do we have time to go there and spend just a little time?" Sally asked. She loved English literature and knew she would never get back there.

"Sure, we can spend as much time as you want," Adam said. "The race isn't until tomorrow."

"This is like driving into a picture book," Sally said as they drove into the quaint town.

"It is kind of cute," Hal said looking at the shops and houses. Vic was quiet but he was looking in every direction taking it all in.

"Adam, pull over if you can," Sally cried. "There's a tourist center."

Sally ran in while the guys looked around outside.

"I got a map," Sally said holding it open for the guys to see. "The clerk said we could walk to most of the places I want to see if you park at the Royal Shakespeare Theatre."

Adam found a good spot and pulled the car in and locked it. Since they had passed many of the places on Sally's list, Hal decided he was going to sit and enjoy the sunshine while they took their walk. The theatre was right along the river Avon and had several gardens around it. Hal walked around there a little while and just knew those gardens had to be beautiful in the summer since there were still so well kept in the dead of winter.

When Hal came back from his garden walk he sat next to a gentleman on one of the many benches.

"Afternoon," Hal said to the man.

"Good afternoon," the gentleman replied. "You are from America?"

"Yes, sir," Hal said proudly. Then extending his hand, he introduced himself. "Hal Graves at your service."

"Avery Kislingbury," Avery replied. "I'm most happy to make your acquaintance."

"You from this town, here?" Hal asked.

"Yes, sir," Avery replied. "Born and raised here and I'll probably be laid to rest here, also."

"That's kind of the way I feel about my town," Hal said. "I'm from a small town in Illinois."

"Are you near Chicago?" Avery asked.

"No, sir," Hal said kind of aggravated that people only think of Chicago when they hear of Illinois. "You ever hear of a town called Hannibal, Missouri?"

“Why yes, of course,” Avery said. “Your Mr. Samuel Clemens wrote of that town.”

“We call him Mark Twain,” Hal said. “But anyway, we live just across the river from Hannibal…except we’re in Illinois.”

“So you are quite south from Chicago then,” Avery said.

“Yes, sir,” Hal said thinking finally someone who knows Illinois geography.

“Are you here alone on holiday?” Avery asked.

“No, there’s my group down the way,” Hal pointed toward the others about two blocks down.

“Sally saw the sign and wanted to stop to visit Shakespeare’s home,” Hal said. “We are actually going to the Formula One races in Manchester tomorrow afternoon.”

“You enjoy the auto races then,” Avery said.

“Yeah, me and the boy are fixing up a car for the stock car races for next year,” Hal said beaming. “We have a 350 late model stock car. She’s a sweetheart.”

“I’ve always wanted to see the American stock car races,” Avery said.

“Well, you should come over and watch us win a few next summer,” Hal said.

“I would love to come,” Avery said. “You’ll have to give me your card.”

“We don’t have them yet, but let me give you my info,” Hal said. As he pulled out his personal card for Avery, the Englishman asked Hal where they were staying.

“Don’t know yet,” Hal said. “We just pulled off the road.”

“I think the youngster would enjoy staying in a castle,” Avery said. “Take my card to the Ettington Park. It’s just a few kilometers south of here. Tell them I sent you and you’ll be set for the night.”

“Thanks, Avery,” Hal said. “Hey, we’ll be looking for you. I’ll send you our schedule and keep you up to date on how the car is coming along.”

“I’d like that,” Avery said as he got up to leave. “Have a good afternoon, Hal.”

“You, too, Avery,” Hal said as he looked at Avery’s business card. There was nothing special about it except his name and information. Nothing about a business was on it.

“Who was that guy you were talking to?” Adam asked Hal as they were walking back to the car.

"A very nice Englishman," Hal said. "He gave me his card and told me to go to this hotel for tonight. He seemed real interested in racing, too. Shall we give the hotel a try?"

"Might as well," Adam said. "We didn't have anything else arranged and it is a little late to try to find one now."

"Look at that!" Vic cried when he saw the castle appear in front of them.

"Jesus, Hal," Adam cried. "We won't be able to afford this."

"Avery said it was quite reasonable," Hal said using his best English accent.

"It better be," Adam said as Vic jumped out of the car not waiting for the valet to open the door. Sally yelled at him to wait.

Sally grabbed Vic's hand after she stepped out of the car and held on to him while he just looked up at the grandeur of the castle. It was magnificent. One of the valets took Sally's camera and got a shot of the four of them in front of the monstrous entry of the hotel before they went in.

Hal walked up to the desk and told the clerk that Mr. Avery Kislingbury had sent them and showed him Mr. Kislingbury's card. The clerk came to attention and tapped on a bell. A bellboy ran toward them and stopped at attention in front of the desk next to Hal.

"Mr. Kislingbury's guests have arrived," the clerk announced.

Without a word, another bellboy arrived and picked up Hal and Sally's bags, while the first one picked up Vic's bags and offered to take Adam's bag.

"That's all right. I can carry this," Adam said with the dollar signs spinning in the back of his mind. Adam hung behind the group for just a moment to talk to the clerk.

"Don't you need my credit card or something?" He asked the desk clerk.

"No, sir," the clerk responded as his face turned red. "Mr. Kislingbury has everything taken care of for you. If there is anything at all you need, please let us know. Enjoy your stay."

Adam was totally confused, but truly happy that their bill was taken care of. He caught up with the group just as the elevator door was opening.

The bellboy opened the double doors to the suite and allowed the group to enter. All four of them were awestruck by the luxury and beauty of the place. Vic was afraid to move for fear of breaking something but he looked at the frescos on the ceiling, the huge paintings on the wall, the heavy Persian Rugs on the floor.

"There's no bed in here," Vic whispered to Adam.

"I know," Adam said.

The bellboy walked over to more double doors and opened them. In front of them were more doors. He showed them to the left was a smaller bedroom with just a double bed. In front of the big doors was another set of double doors that led into a master bedroom with a king size bed. There was a bathroom off of this bedroom with a beautiful claw foot tub and a shower. Across from the other bedroom was one identical to it with a double bed. A door next to this room led to another bathroom.

The bellboy then showed the group where there were drinks and snacks behind the bar. He showed Hal how to operate the television and told Adam that the hotel was computer ready. Hal reached into his pocket to tip the bellboys, but they both declined saying it had been taken care of.

"I don't know who you met, but he must be a close friend of Santa Claus," Adam said.

"Got that right," Hal said.

Vic ran and jumped on the big bed, but was immediately scolded by Sally.

"This is where I'm sleeping," Vic said as he rolled around the big bed.

"Do you snore?" Adam said as he jumped on top of the boy scaring him.

"I don't think so," Vic said.

"OK, you can stay," Adam said as he climbed off the big bed.

"You sure about this?" Sally asked Adam.

"Well, I sure as hell ain't sleeping with Hal," Adam said seriously. "And I doubt if you'll sleep with me." Sally's cheeks got all rosy. "So I don't have any other choice now do I."

Hal came walking in about that time.

"I just looked at those snacks," he said. "Ain't much to fill up a man's stomach. Anyone ready to go eat supper?"

"I'd just like to stay here," Sally said. "After traveling, I'm really tired."

"Yeah, me too," Adam said. "We can go down to the restaurant and see what they offer."

"Fine with me," Hal said.

"Me, too," Vic said. "Let's go."

Down in the restaurant, the group looked at the menu and couldn't figure out half of the things offered.

"I thought they spoke English in this country," Hal complained looking at the menu items.

"They do," Adam said but agreeing with Hal that the menu sure didn't look English.

The waitress came over to take their order and could tell they were confused.

"May I help you order?" She asked.

"Do you have anything simple?" Sally asked. "We've been traveling all day and I just want something simple so I can go up and go to sleep."

"Do you want a meal or just a sandwich?" The waitress asked. "Or right now, we have some very good soups for the winter."

"Oh, soup sounds real good," Sally said. "What kind of soup?"

"Our specialty is potato soup," the waitress said. It is a cream soup with chunks of potato with onion, carrots and celery. We can serve it in a bread bowl, or a cup."

"Is this venison stew with potatoes, carrots and onions, too?" Adam asked.

"Oh, yes sir," she replied. "That is served also in our bread bowl, or we can put it on a sandwich for you. Both of these are very filling."

"I want the soup, but I don't want the bread but I want more than a cup," Hal said.

"Not a problem, sir," the waitress said writing down his order. "We also serve soup in bowls. Would you like a sandwich with that or some venison sausage and cheese perhaps?"

"Yeah, that sounds good," Hal said putting his menu down.

"I think I'll have the stew on bread, please," Adam said as he passed his menu to Hal.

Sally ordered a cup of soup with the sausage then looked over to Vic.

"What's the matter?" She asked him when he didn't order.

"I want both of them," Vic said with a sad look on his face.

"We can do a half order of stew and a cup of soup," the waitress offered her suggestion.

"That will be fine," Sally said getting a big smile from Vic.

"So buddy, are you having fun yet," Adam asked Vic as the boy was leaning his head on his hand.

"Yea, but I'm getting kind of tired," Vic said.

"Well, hang in there because tomorrow is going to be a big day," Adam said ruffling the lad's hair.

Hal was just putting down his spoon from taking the last bite of his soup when he looked up and saw Avery Kislingbury walk into the restaurant. Avery walked over between Hal and Adam and before Adam could stand to greet the older gentleman, Avery put his hand on his shoulder.

"Don't let me interrupt your meal," Avery said. "I just came to check on your accommodations and make sure everything is acceptable for you."

"Oh, my yes," Hal said. "We weren't expecting to your guests."

"No, sir," Adam said. "We expect to pay our way."

"Entertain an old man," Avery said. "I did enjoy our conversation this afternoon and do look forward to seeing you race next summer."

"Sit down, Avery," Hal ordered as he pulled up a chair. "Makes my neck hurt looking up."

Avery laughed as he sat down between the two men.

"Do you have any plans after the race tomorrow?" Avery asked looking toward Adam.

"Yes, sir," Adam said. "We are going over to Kings Lynn for the race on Sunday."

"Ah, splendid," Avery leaned back and clapped his hands together. "I was going to invite you to come to my box at the raceway there. Most of my mates that go with me are off on holiday now and I do hate to go alone."

"Can we go in the pits?" Vic asked innocently.

"Victor," Sally cried out to her son.

"As a matter of fact, we could probably go into the crew area," Avery said. "I'm sorry, Sally, but ladies are not allowed."

"It's the same at home, too," Sally said.

"Well, I am going to leave your tickets at the desk and I will see you at Kings Lynn," Avery said. "I'm so very excited."

"Thanks so much, Avery," Adam said. "We'll see you then."

The next morning the group got up, showered, ate breakfast and took off for Belle Vue. There was a lot of activity around the speedway and Adam had a hard time finding a place to park. He finally saw a police officer and asked him about parking and was directed to a Car Park…what they call parking lots…near the speedway.

"I swear we passed this five times and I never saw it," Adam said as he turned in.

It felt good getting back into a raceway again. The sounds, the smells and the whole atmosphere put Adam in a good mood. Vic was holding on to Adam's hand and looking around at everything. There was more seating, more vendors and even pit road seemed longer.

Their seats were right along pit road so they had to cross through the tunnel to the infield. There was a lot of activity in the infield and the drivers were just getting out of their meeting when the group came toward the concessions.

"Look, Adam," Vic cried pointing out all the drivers. "Do you know any of them?"

"No, buddy," Adam said looking at all the guys. "These are all English drivers."

"They look just like us though," Vic said. Adam smiled and nodded.

Some of the heat races had already started by the time the group had found their seats. Vic couldn't sit still. He hadn't picked out his favorite, yet. He kept looking though the program, then watching who was on the track. He had his watch with him and timed a driver whose car he liked then did the same with another. He was taking this very serious. Sally was so thrilled she agreed to let him come along.

They watched race after race and Vic yelled as if he were at home and his favorite driver was in each race. He read stats to Adam and Hal and told them about the points that the winner received off of each race. He was so into it.

"Mr. Hal Graves?" An usher asked Hal between races.

"I'm Graves," Hal said.

"We received a message for you from Mr. Kislingbury," the usher said. "He asked you call him at this number." The usher handed Hal a cell phone and waited.

"Hal, I was hoping they would find you," Avery said when Hal called.

Avery invited them to drive over to Kings Lynn after the race and stay with him at his Hillington Estate. When Hal agreed he was told the usher had a map.

“Splendid,” Avery said. “We will be expecting you late this evening. Keep the phone and call if you have any problems.”

Hal thanked him and assured him they would see him later.

During the third race there was a little excitement when two cars touched and one skidded into the wall. The car was not seriously damaged, but it did give cause for the yellow flag and the car limped around the track before coming into pit road and resigning the race.

“I don’t think they are as aggressive as we are,” Adam said to Hal after the race was over.

“They drive like gentlemen,” Hal said with a laugh.

“They aren’t as fast as we are either,” Vic said as he was waiting for the feature.

“You sure about that, Vic?” Adam asked looking at Vic’s stats.

“Yeah,” Vic pointed out the speeds of the last several races. “They’re about 10 miles an hour slower than at home.”

“He’s right,” Adam said as he showed Hal the stats.

“No wonder it’s not been so exciting,” Hal said with a laugh.

The feature was a pretty good race. They had a full slate and the cars were fighting to come to the front. The lead cars pulled away from the pack almost immediately, but there was a car, number 5, from the middle of the pack passing everyone weaving in and around traffic. He soon caught up with the front bunch of cars and tried to pass them. But they were working together and wouldn’t let him pass. This went on for a few laps and as soon as the lead car took a pit stop, the car number 5 slipped around two of the lead cars then dropped down and passed the lead car on the inside. He flew down the straightaway and started lapping the other cars fighting his way back through the bunch of cars. This time the pack from the back stuck together and wouldn’t let the other cars lap them. The crowd was going wild.

The cars moved aside for number 5 and he sped past everyone and finally caught up with the lead cars that were still trying to lap the big group. He eased around one and lapped him. With the help of some of his friends, he lapped the other one. And with one lap to go, he snuck by the third car. He was a full lap ahead of his closest competitor. He flew by the rest of the pack as they closed up the gap behind him holding the others at bay. Vic was on his feet as were the rest of the fans. He had his watch out and punched the button to see how fast he truly was going. Around he went, seeing the starter holding the checkered flag high above his head. Around the final curve he came and down the straightaway and pass the finish line.

Vic was screaming as if he had see Jeff Gordon win the championship. He was pounding on Adam's arm and hugging his mom.

"I've never seen such a race," Hal said when they were on their way to Avery's estate.

"It was different, for sure," Adam said. "I never saw such big gaps."

"Well he was lapping all of them," Hal said laughing.

"It almost looked like it was a fixed race," Adam said. "What do you think?"

"Naw, he was getting the blue flag," Hal said. "They had to give him room."

"I guess you're right," Adam said. "I doubt if our drivers would give up that much of the track for anyone though." Hal nodded.

Adam pulled into the circular drive of Avery's Hillington Estate. It was a grand three story Country Mansion. As soon as the car stopped at the front door, a man stepped out to help with the bags and lead the group into the house. Vic looked around at all of the beautiful pictures on the wall and pretty things sitting around. Sally leaned over and warned him not to touch anything. Vic walked over close to Adam.

"Who is this guy?" Adam whispered to Hal. He just shrugged his shoulders.

"Ah, I hope you had a good drive," Avery said as he walked into the hall with his arms extended. "Welcome to Hillington. Please come sit for a few minutes."

"You have a lovely home, Mr. Kislingbury," Sally said as they walked into the parlor.

"Thank you, Mrs. Cooper, we like it here," Avery said. "Would any of you like something to eat, some tea, coffee, wine?" Vic leaned over and whispered to Adam that he was hungry. Avery heard him.

"Would you like something to eat, Vic?" Avery asked him. Vic nodded and then looked at his mom. Sally nodded as her stomach growled at that moment. "Sounds like someone else might need some nourishment, also." Avery smiled and walked back toward the kitchen of the house. The same man that carried in their luggage met him at the door and Avery said something to him. Then Avery came back to the living room and sat back down.

"We'll have something for you in a few moments," he said.

And it was just a few minutes when the butler walked back out and stood at attention, waited for Avery to recognize him before he said, "Supper is served." Then he turned on his heel and simply walked back to the kitchen.

After a light supper and a little more conversation, everyone was shown to their rooms. Adam took Vic to his room and told him that Sally was going to be next door and that he was going to across the hall. Vic was OK with that. Adam helped Vic take off his shoes and led him to the bathroom one last time so he knew where it was in case he had to get up in the middle of the night. Vic kicked his jeans off and left them lay on the floor. Adam made him pick them up and put them on a chair which he did.

"Good night, Adam." Vic called from under the big featherbed. "I love you."

"Night, buddy," Adam said feeling a lump in his throat. "Love you, too." Adam closed the door and stood in the hallway for just a moment before going to his own room. This is what he is supposed to feel with his own family, he thought.

The next morning Adam, Sally and Hal were awaken by taps on their door. Adam woke up Vic and they were told breakfast would be served in a half an hour.

When they were seated around the table being served a delicious breakfast of omelets and muffins with tea or coffee, Avery made an announcement.

"My niece Pamela is coming with us to the race. She enjoys them, but doesn't care about going with just me. When I told her that you, Sally, were accompanying us, she was thrilled."

"I'm happy she's going along," Sally said.

"I'm sorry to keep you waiting, Uncle," Pamela said as she walked into the dining room.

Adam and Hal stood up when she entered. Adam nudged Vic to get him on his feet.

Pamela was a very pretty woman in her late 20's. She seemed

over dressed to be going to the races, but then again, they were in England. She had on a very dressy ivory linen pant suit over a blouse with dark green ruffled blouse. She also wore a pretty green hat with an ivory band around the brim.

When everyone was finished with their meal and had enough coffee or tea, Avery was ready to get started. He wanted to go early so they could visit with the crews.

"Are we all ready to go now?" Avery asked directing the question to Pamela rather than to everyone. She nodded.

"Wow you can see the whole track from here," Vic cried when they were escorted into Avery's luxury box. There were several seats along the glass wall facing the race track, but behind those it looked like a sitting room with sofas, comfortable chairs, a dining area, bar and even a gaming table.

"Would you like to go to the garage area?" Avery asked Vic glancing over to the older men.

"You betcha," Vic cried as he grabbed Adam's hand.

"Have fun," Pamela called after them. Then to Sally she said, "Let the boys have their toys."

Sally smiled.

Hal and Adam were amazed at the garage area here. It was spotless. There were no oil or grease spots on the floor. It even smelled different from the pits at home. They didn't hear the whine of the hydraulic screw drivers or a lot of talking. There were no sparks from welders. No radios blasting the latest country songs. It was pretty quiet.

They walked down the aisle between the cars and Vic looked at all the Formula One cars on either side of them. The cars were smaller and even shaped differently than the black beauty waiting for them at home. Vic was amazed how the cars carried the wing on top. He pointed it out to Adam as they were walking and the two of them laughed at how funny they looked.

The group stopped at the pit of KISCO Race Team. Avery walked over and talked to one of the mechanics before the two of them walked back to Adam, Hal and Vic.

Avery introduced his head mechanic, Colin Ettington.

"You have something to do with that hotel we stayed in the other night?" Hal asked. Colin nodded.

"That is my uncle's hotel," Colin said. "I hope you were comfortable there."

"Yeah, it was a nice place," Hal said. "Avery made sure we didn't need a thing."

"So are you an owner, Avery?" Adam asked their host.

"I am that," Avery said. "Colin and I are partners thereby the name. We actually have four cars we are entering today."

Adam looked around and noticed all the crews in the same color jumpsuits. They were working between the four different cars. It seemed strange that one car didn't have just one team. He mentioned that to Avery.

"We have our engine crew, our tire crew, etc.," Avery said. "They are the best at what they do and they can work on all the cars. They do their very best for the team because they get paid no matter which car wins."

"Makes sense," Adam said. He noticed Vic was inching closer and closer to the cars. "Vic!"

Vic turned quickly and stepped back next to Adam.

"Would the lad like to see one up close?" Avery asked Adam. Then he looked at Vic. The lad nodded his head and smiled.

"Sure would," Vic said. Adam nudged him lightly. "Thank you," Vic added.

Avery took Adam and Vic over near one of the cars that no one was working on at the moment. Vic stood about a foot away from it, mouth wide open in awe. He stretched to see inside and looked at the dashboard.

"Go on, lad, take a good look," Avery ordered him. Vic looked up at Adam before stepping closer. Adam nodded.

Vic crept up to the car and touched the open window and looked in. The steering wheel was sitting on the seat so he could see all the dials. His eyes got very big all of a sudden. He pulled out and went over to Adam and pulled him down to whisper in Adam's ear.

"Their speedometers go up to 300," Vic yelled in a whisper that was cracking his voice.

Adam stood up and laughed at him.

"Those aren't miles per hour on there," Adam said. Then he tried to explain the difference between kilometers and miles. After a few minutes, he finally got Vic straightened out and he felt better that the

English didn't have faster cars than we do.

Both Adam and Vic were interested to see under the hood. It had a simple 8 cylinder 350 engine and a 4 barrel carburetor. It was sweet. Adam looked up and Avery and Hal were talking about fuel mixtures and tire pressure.

"I hope you're learning something," Adam said as the two walked over to the car."

"Indeed, we are both learning from each other," Avery said clamping his hand on Hal's shoulder. Then to Vic, he asked, "Are you ready to meet some drivers?" Vic's eyes popped and he just stood there. Adam nudged him again and he nodded. The men laughed at the boy.

Avery handed Vic a program and walked around with him to get autographs from his drivers. Adam and Hal talked to them, while Colin brought in a few of the other drivers for Vic to meet. Some of the drivers were actually interested in meeting Adam and Hal, too.

"I wish I would have had some business cards made up before we left," Hal said as they walked back to the box.

"Who knew," Adam said keeping hold of Vic as he was looking all over and wandering off from time to time.

Today's race was a lot faster and much more exciting than the one they saw yesterday. The cars went up on two wheels as they went around the curves. Every now and then, a car would tap another and the crowd went wild. By the end of the day two of Avery's cars won their heats and both placed in the top three in the feature. He was satisfied with the outcome, but not thrilled.

"Uncle usually has a victory celebration when they win the feature," Pamela said. "He so wanted to have that for you."

"Things happen," Adam said as they got up to leave. Pamela slipped her arm through Adam's arm as they began their trek to the car. Vic didn't like that and he walked over and broke it up and took Adam's hand.

"Excuse me," Pamela cried. "What a rude little bugger."

"Excuse you, too," Adam said with a scowl on his face. "He's been told to stay with me. He's my special buddy."

"Well, he's still a rude little retard," Pamela said as she started walking away.

Adam grabbed her arm and whipped her around until she was face to face with him.

"Don't you ever call him or anyone that," Adam said in a very stern soft voice that scared Pamela. "For the grace of God…"

Adam let go of Pamela's arm and she just stood there as he and Vic walked away. Sally saw what had just happened. When Sally walked by, she looked at Pamela and did not say a word or give her any specific look. A tear rolled down Pamela's cheek.

"I'm sorry, Sally," Pamela said softly. Sally turned toward the rest and walked out. It was only then, when she was alone, that Pamela followed the group to the car.

Adam led a sleepy Vic to his bedroom as soon as they arrived back at Avery's home. The boy could barely make it up to his room as he was half asleep.

"Vic, wake up and look at me," Adam yelled to the comatose boy.

"I'm tired, Adam," Vic said leaning onto Adam's chest.

"I know, but wake up for just a minute," Adam ordered him as he pushed Vic upright and took his face in his hands.

"What," Vic said looking at Adam through half open eyes.

"Vic, look around you," Adam ordered as the boy looked around the room. "We're at Avery's house. This is your room tonight. Your mom is right through that door. And I am across the hall." Vic started to drop his head. "Vic, are you listening to me?" Adam asked as he shook the boy a little.

"Yeah, mom over there and you in hall," Vic mumbled. "I'm tired."

Adam helped take off Vic's shoes and jeans and the boy crawled in the big bed after going to the bathroom one last time. He was asleep before his head hit the pillow.

"Thanks, Adam," Sally said. "He had such a busy day."

"He had a great day," Adam said. "I made him tell me where he was and where we are going to be. I hope he'll be OK if he wakes up."

The house was very quiet and the light from the moon was shining across Vic's bed. He woke up and remembered where he was and rolled over to go back to sleep. He saw a little girl sitting in the window seat looking at him. He sat up in bed and looked over to her.

"Who are you?" Vic asked the girl who was dressed in a pretty pink party dress. Her long dark hair was pulled back on both sides held by pink ribbons. She looked like she could have been Vic's age or a year or so older. She was very pretty, but looked sad.

"Regan," she replied quietly.

"Hi, Regan, I'm Vic," he replied introducing himself. "Is this your room?"

"It used to be," she said not moving from her seat.

"I didn't mean to take your room," Vic said as he got out of bed and walked over to sit next to her. Regan giggled at him. Vic had forgotten that he was just wearing his underwear so he quickly grabbed a blanket off the bed and wrapped it around his legs before sitting on the other end of the window seat. "Sorry," he said.

"You can use my room," Regan said. "Not many people do anymore. They are afraid of me."

"Why? You're so pretty," Vic said not understanding what he was seeing.

"Where's your mom and dad?" Vic continued.

"My mum lives here most of the time," Regan said. "I don't know where my father is." Regan lowered her head and a tear rolled down her cheek.

The door opened then and Sally walked in.

"Victor, what on earth are you doing?" Sally said walking over to her son.

"I'm talking to Regan," Vic said as he pointed to an empty spot on the window seat.

"You get your body back in that bed," Sally ordered. "We have a very busy day tomorrow."

"But, Mom," Vic protested. "She needs somebody to talk to. Can't you see her?"

"Don't be a silly goose," Sally said. "Now go back to sleep." Sally tucked her son in bed, gave him a kiss and went back to her room.

"I'm sorry I got you in trouble," Regan whispered sitting on the edge of the bed.

"Yeah, she gets pretty mad sometimes," Vic whispered leaning on his elbow looking at Regan.

"We're going to London tomorrow," Vic whispered with excitement.

"Oh, I did so love going there," Regan cried softly. "It is so beautiful. Are you going to see Buckingham Palace?"

"I don't know," Vic whispered very interested in what Regan had to say.

"Do try to go when they have the changing of the guard," she said. "I always tried to make one of the Beefeaters laugh." Regan giggled. "They are so serious."

"We're going to see Big Ben," Vic whispered.

"Splendid," Regan said. "That's in the Tower of London you know."

"I better go back to sleep so I can stay awake for all that tomorrow," Vic whispered. "I like you Regan. Can we write to each other when I go home?"

"I wish I could," Regan said lowering her head.

"That's OK," Vic said thinking she didn't know how. "Good night!"

"Good Night, Vic," Regan said as she got up from the bed. She stood at the side of the bed until Vic was asleep. Then she simply turned and walked over to the window seat to stare out at the moon.

After everyone was awaken by Avery's manservant and told breakfast would be in a half an hour, Vic got his pants and shoes on and came running down the large staircase to the parlor. Adam was already there drinking some tea and looking out over the frosty wintery grounds of the estate.

"I bet this place is fantastic in the summer," Adam said under his breath.

"Adam are we going to Bucking Palace today?" Vic asked.

"You mean Buckingham Palace?" Adam corrected the lad. "I guess we could if we can find it. How do you know about Buckingham Palace?"

"Regan told me about it last night," Vic said innocently.

There was a crash behind them. When they turned around Pamela was standing but her cup of tea had shattered when she dropped it upon hearing Vic's statement.

"Are you all right?" Adam asked her as he could see she was physically upset. He led Pamela over to one of the sofas and sat down next to her. She was shaken, looking at Vic.

"You saw Regan last night?" Pamela asked Vic. He nodded. "You talked to her, too?" Vic nodded again. He thought he was in trouble and moved closer to Adam.

"Who's Regan?" Adam asked Pamela. She began to cry.

"Regan is my daughter," Pamela said through her tears. "Or, I should say, she was my daughter."

Avery walked in about that time, saw the maid cleaning up the mess and wondered what had happened.

"What is it, niece?" Avery asked Pamela walking over to her and sitting down.

Pamela grabbed Avery and buried her face in his sweater. Avery looked at Adam.

"Vic said he saw Regan last night," Adam said.

"Oh my word," Avery said as he embraced his niece tighter.

Both Adam and Vic looked confused. Hal and Sally came in then to the upsetting sight. Adam got up and walked over to them.

"Vic said he saw Pamela's dead daughter last night," Adam told them quietly.

"That's who he was talking to," Sally said now realizing why Vic was out of bed in the middle of the night. The men looked confused. "I heard him talking in his room so I got up to put him back to bed. He fussed with me that he was talking to somebody named Regan. That must have been the daughter's name." Adam nodded.

They had noticed that Vic was sitting close to Pamela so they walked closer to hear what she was saying to him.

"So you saw the little girl?" Pamela asked Vic. He nodded looking scared. Adam walked over by Vic assuring him he was not in trouble.

"What did she look like?" Pamela asked.

"She's very pretty," Vic beamed. "She was dressed to go to a party with pretty ribbons in her hair. Are you her mom?" Pamela nodded.

"Did she look happy?" Pamela asked tears dropping onto her cheeks.

"Sometimes," Vic said. "When we talked about the meat eaters we laughed. But she said she misses going to London and she misses her dad."

"Oh my word," Avery said as he stood up and walked to the window.

Sally walked over to Avery seeing he was upset. He had tears in his eyes, too.

"Oh, Sally, we've had guests tell us they had seen Regan, but nothing like this," Avery said. "I brushed it off as a fluke, or a tease.

But this is real. How could Vic know these things, if she had not talked to him?"

"Vic is an innocent," Sally said. Avery nodded.

"Sally, it was so sad," Avery started. "We had just come in from the hunt. Mason was putting his guns away and had them lying on the table. He had forgotten to unload one of them and when he picked it up it went off and shot his daughter. It was an accident, but he blamed himself. He and Pamela's marriage suffered greatly for it even though she did not blame him. She was their life."

"Where is Mason now?" Sally asked.

"He is gone," Avery said. "About a year ago now, he put the same gun in his mouth."

"Oh my," Sally gasped. "I'm so sorry."

"He was a good lad," Avery said. "Pamela truly loved him still. She would have taken him back in a second. Losing him so soon after Regan…well, it was very difficult."

Avery and Sally looked over to Pamela and Vic.

"You are a very special boy," Pamela said as she got up and walked to a desk at the side of the room. Walking back over to Vic, she handed him a picture of Regan wearing the same pink ribbons in her hair. "I'd like you to have this."

"Mom, look," Vic cried holding the picture up as he walked toward Sally. "This is her. This is Regan that I was talking to when you came in last night."

"What do you say?" Sally whispered. Vic turned around to Pamela.

"Thank you," Vic said as he looked at the picture. "She looks just like this."

"She's very pretty," Sally said looking at the sweet innocent face.

"She's my friend in England," Vic said still not understanding what she is. "I wish I could write to her, but she said she didn't think she could."

"You write to her," Pamela said knowing Vic didn't understand. "I'll make sure she writes you back. Do you have email?" Vic nodded. "That will be the best way."

Vic was so thrilled he had a new email friend…in England no less!

After breakfast the Americans packed the car and were ready to take the two hour trip to London. They truly hated to leave their new English friends, but Avery promised he would see them next summer when Adam started racing. He and Hal had exchanged so much information that they knew they would stay friends and perhaps become business partners. Even Colin, KISCO's chief mechanic wanted to get involved in American racing, so he might tag along.

The good-byes were bittersweet, but Avery promised the months would go by quickly. And, Pamela told Vic to be sure to let them know how things are going with the black beauty.

Avery and Pamela stood on the stoop of the mansion until the car turned onto the highway.

"Nice people," Avery said as they turned to go into the house.

Chapter 9

The trip through the English countryside was uneventful and somewhat boring as the landscape was winter worn gray and brown. They were not fifteen minutes into the trip when Vic leaned against him mom and fell asleep. The towns and houses they passed were few and held no interest for them to stop. They wanted to get to London, find a place to stay and then begin seeing the sites.

Adam drove straight to Trafalgar Square and pulled into a parking garage near the May Fair. After they checked in the first thing Vic wanted to do was eat. So they went to a deli they saw on the way in called Delitaly and had a nice lunch before venturing out to see some of the sites of the city. Vic found a book store close by and ran in and bought a guide book showing all the attractions of the city. Of course, he immediately looked up the Tower of London and Big Ben.

"When can we go see this?" Vic pointed to the clock in the book.

"How about right now?" Adam said making the boy grin.

Hal looked at the map and figured he'd never get back to London so he decided to hobble along. They walked slowly and Vic was reading the history of the tower and the clock as they walked. Sally kept her hand on his elbow guiding him as he read.

"The tower has been used as a prison, palace and place of execution, arsenal, mint and menagerie, since its construction following the Norman Conquest of 1066," Vic read from the guide book. "Wow! That's almost a thousand years old!" Vic was amazed as he went back to his book.

After another block of walking, Sally tapped Vic on the shoulder and pointed ahead of him. He looked toward the edge of her finger and there was the clock tower looming in front of him.

"Whoa!" Vic cooed as he stared ahead at the tower against the bright blue sky.

Adam looked at the clock and it was just a minute or so before noon. They started walking quickly as Vic wanted to get to the tower as soon as he could. They were about a block away from the clock when they heard the first chime. Vic stopped and looked up at his mom. The second bell rang and he looked at Hal. When the third bell rang he looked at Adam. The chimes continued. He clapped his hands and jumped up and down. Then there was a pause. All of a sudden Big Ben started announcing the hour.

"Bong! Bang! Bong!"

Vic covered his ears laughing still bouncing. The bell was very loud. When it finished, Vic put his hand on his stomach.

"I could feel the sound in my tummy," he said still laughing. "That was so cool."

Sally was so tickled watching her son enjoy the sound of the bells. He thought the clock itself was Big Ben. Now he knew that the bell was Big Ben and he knew why it received the name.

They went through the tower and Vic got everything he could about the tower, the clock, and Big Ben.

On the way back to the Jewel Tower they stopped and went to Westminster Abbey. Sally was in awe at how big and beautiful it was. She got chills thinking this is where kings and queens had walked. And remembered watching Prince Charles and Diana's wedding on television. It looked so much bigger in person. She didn't realize she had tears in her eyes. Adam walked up and put his arm around her waist.

"Are you all right?" He whispered startling her. She wiped her eyes and smiled.

"Yes," Sally smiled at Adam. "It's just so amazingly beautiful. Thank you for bringing Vic and me."

Adam gave her a little squeeze and walked back over to Vic and Hal who were sitting in one of the pews resting.

"You know all the kings are crowned here and some of the kings and queens are buried here," Vic said reading from his book. "It was started by Benedictine monks in the tenth century," Vic looked up counting on his fingers. "Is that a thousand years?" Adam nodded. "Wow! This is as old as the clock tower."

They started walking toward Parliament Street on their way to Trafalgar Square. Again Vic had his nose in the book looking for sites along the street on the map. He'd look down at the map and up around him and then down again. After a little way, he stopped and looked at a street sign. Everyone stopped waiting for a big announcement. He pointed to the street sign.

"Their Prime Minister lives here," Vic said pointing to the Downing Street sign. Then looking at his companions he asked, "Is that like the preacher for the church?" They laughed.

Sally explained to him it was like our president. Vic became excited them hoping to see something like our White House. They turned and walked a short way and saw a common looking house with the number 10 on the outside.

"That's it?" Vic cried terribly disappointed. Then thinking a minute, he said, "Their country is a lot smaller than America. I bet they can't afford anything much better." The adults stifled their laughter and just smiled at him.

A couple blocks farther Vic stopped again and looked over to his right. He turned the corner and took a few steps. Right in front of them was Scotland Yard.

"Well, I'll be," Hal said. "We got ourselves a bloodhound."

They walked around looking at the building watching the English policemen going in and out. They turned and continued their trek to Trafalgar Square. Sally was amazed at the architecture and age of the old buildings. A short walk and they saw the monument in the middle of the square. Hal saw a bench near a bus stop and sat down. He was getting very tired. Sally looked over Vic's shoulder.

"How about going across the square to the National Gallery and you can rest, Hal," Sally suggested as she pointed just across the square to the large building. Hal nodded as he got up and started along.

"You going to be all right?" Adam asked him as he was truly slowing down.

"Yeah," Hal said wheezing. "I can't remember the last time I've walked this much. But I sure don't want to miss out. I'll probably never get back here." Hal looked up at Adam with a painful smile.

Once they reached the museum, Hal sat just inside while the others started walking through. Again, Vic had to get a book of the exhibits. He stopped at each painting and if he liked it, he would look it up in the book and read about the painting and the artist before moving on.

A couple hours later they came back to find Hal sitting with his arms across his chest and his chin resting on his chest. He was sleeping. Adam leaned down and touched him gently on his shoulder.

"Hal," Adam said softly. Hal lifted his head and opened his eyes stretching his arms.

"I must've dozed off," he said. "Anyone know where a john is around here?"

They all agreed it was about time to find a place to go and Vic looked in his book to find one.

"What would we do without you?" Hal said as they walked out of the building relieved and ready to go again on their adventure. Vic was so proud.

"Anybody hungry?" Adam asked as he looked at his watch seeing it was getting close to 5:30. Of course, Vic said he was. They got out his guide book and found an interesting place called Café In the Crypt that was nearby. They walked just a little over a block or so and found it. It looked fancier than it sounded but they decided to try it anyway. It was a fun place to eat.

While they were eating dessert it was decided that they would take a taxi back to the hotel. Hal had walked an awfully lot today and he was pretty tired. He was so happy to hear they were taking a taxi that he picked up the tab for supper.

When they got back to the hotel Hal went right to bed. Vic took his bath in the old claw foot tub then crawled under the feather bed in the bed he was sharing with Adam. Sally came out to the living room where Adam was sitting on the sofa looking though Vic's guide book.

"He was asleep as soon as I pulled the covers up," Sally said sitting at the other end of the sofa. "I still can't thank you enough for bringing us along. We are both having such a good time."

"And you were worried about Vic," Adam said.

"He's been good because you've been here," Sally said. "He likes you so much."

"He's a good kid," Adam said smiling. Then looking at the book, he asked Sally, "Anything you want to do tomorrow?"

"Well, Vic has his heart set on seeing Bucking Palace and the meat eaters," Sally said laughing.

"We'll be sure to do that," Adam said looking back at the book.

"What are the chances of going to Stonehenge?" Sally asked.

"They say it is an hour and a half from London," Adam said as he was reading the information from the book. "I guess we could go if you really want to."

"If we can't, that's OK," Sally said getting up and walking toward the closet. She pulled out a bottle of water. "Do you want one?" She asked Adam. He shook his head.

Adam pulled out his laptop to write some emails while Sally went to take a nice soaking bath. When he pulled up his account he had about twenty messages from Ava. He read and answered the others before he checked hers. His parents were very upset that he did not make an effort to come home for Christmas. She said they didn't understand why he had to go to England right then instead of coming to see them. Ava said they grumbled all day and made everyone else's day miserable.

Adam emailed her back and told her not to blame him for their horrible Christmas. He had told the family that he was taking the trip way before the day and they made no fuss about it. He also told Ava they were having a super time. He was very surprised when his cell phone rang within ten minutes after he sent the email.

"Adam, you have no idea how bad it was," Ava cried into the phone. "Dad was especially hateful to the boys. He just pretty much ignored the rest of us."

"What do you mean, he was hateful to the boys?" Adam asked her.

"He threw it back in their faces again," Ava said. "He said it was their fault that you weren't with us. They got into a big fight and Andy left even before we ate." Ava was crying.

"I'm sorry they ruined it for you," Adam said. "It probably wouldn't have been much difference if I would have been there."

"When are you coming home?" Ava asked.

"We'll be back in the states late Thursday, I think," Adam said. "I'm not sure with the time change and all."

"Can we get together over the weekend?" Ava asked.

"Yeah, I'll call you when I get home," Adam said.

After the call Adam was upset with his father that he spoiled the family's Christmas. Why does the old man still hang on to something that happened so long ago? It makes Adam so mad when he thinks about it.

He got up and pushed his chair back so hard it fell backwards. After picking it up he took a deep breath then walked over and got a Pepsi out of the refrigerator. He popped the tab and drank the whole can straight down.

"Are you that thirsty?" Sally said as she walked out rubbing her hair with a towel.

"Let's just say it's a good thing I'm not a drinker right now,"

Adam said sitting back down in front of the computer.

"What happened?" Sally asked as she sat on the sofa wrapping herself in the fluffy white robe.

"My sister told me about the delightful Christmas at the Dieker house," Adam said faking an English accent.

"I take it you're being sarcastic," Sally said starting to brush her shoulder length hair.

"Yeah," Adam said with a laugh. Adam popped another Pepsi and sat in the big chair across from Sally. He told Sally what Ava had told him. Sally looked confused.

"Oh, you don't know the story," Adam said. Adam gave her an abridged version of what happened so many years ago. Then added, "And they still hold it against me."

"That doesn't seem quite fair to me," Sally said. Adam shook his head.

"You think it does to me?" Adam asked her. "I was just as much a victim as they were. I wanted to tell but the old man wouldn't let me. He told me he'd come after me, too."

"Why didn't any of you tell after he was gone?" Sally asked.

"We figured it was over and would never happen again," Adam said. "But Andrew and Aaron hated me because I wouldn't tell to make him stop." Adam looked away. "They didn't know."

"Adam, I'm so sorry," Sally said.

"Mom!" Vic called from the other room.

"I'll get him," Adam said wiping the tears as he walked toward Vic's bedroom.

Several minutes later Adam walked back out to where Sally was sitting.

"He had to go to the bathroom and couldn't remember where it was," Adam said as he sat back down picking up his Pepsi.

"Thanks, Adam," Sally said. "You know, as good as you are with Vic, one would think you had the perfect parents. You're going to make a great Dad, Adam." Adam smiled.

"With Vic, it's easy," Adam said. "If anyone ever did anything to hurt that kid…"

"Yeah, he does that to me, too," Sally said smiling.

The next morning after breakfast the group grabbed a taxi and went over to Buckingham Palace. They had just missed the changing of the guard but Vic got up real close to one of the Beefeaters. He was told he could not touch the guard or anything around him. So, he made funny faces at the guard, burped, shook his behind and even farted. He had Adam, Sally and Hal in stitches but that Beefeater stood stoic and did not flinch.

"The guy must be dead," Hal said laughing at everything Vic was doing.

"They say in the book that they are taught that nothing disturbs them," Sally said.

Vic suddenly stopped and walked over to the huge iron gate. Adam walked over to him.

"Come on, buddy, you can't be here," Adam said.

"Adam," Vic said breathlessly. "Look, up there." Vic was pointing toward the middle of the palace. "There's the king!"

Adam looked but did not see anyone. He looked along all the windows but saw nothing in any of the windows on any of the floors.

"Come on, Vic, there's no one there," Adam said trying to pull the boy away from the gate.

"No, Adam, look," Vic said as he pulled his arm away from Adam's grip. Vic started waving to the man he saw in the window. The man waved back to him.

Sally walked over to Vic.

"Mom, look, there's the king," Vic said still waving.

"Victor, there's no one there," Sally said. "You're acting silly."

Vic looked at his mother with a scowl on his face. Then he looked up and the man waved once more and turned away into the palace.

"You made him leave," Vic said as he turned away from Sally and walked toward Hal. As he passed Adam he snatched the guide book away from Adam. He sat down on the bench next to Hal and opened it to the monarchs. Vic was scanning the pictures of the old kings running his finger down one page and up the other. He finally stopped at a picture of Queen Victoria. "It's a queen," Vic whispered.

"What'd you say, boy?" Hal asked looked over to Vic.

"Nothing," Vic said as he closed the book and looked back toward the castle.

"What's the matter with Vic?" Hal asked Adam and Sally when they walked over to the bench.

"He's mad at us right now," Sally said.

"You made her go away," Vic said as he got up and started

walking back to the gates.

"Oh, it's a she now," Adam said. Hal looked confused. Adam explained that Vic said he saw a king in one of the windows of the palace.

"Well, the boy was looking at his book and said it was a queen," Hal said. "I didn't know what he was talking about."

"I beg your pardon," a British gentleman interrupted their conversation. "Do I understand that the young chap saw Queen Victoria in the palace?"

"He says he did," Sally said. She was going to say something else, but the gentleman spoke first.

"They say that she wanders the corridors," he said. "It's unusual that she showed herself during the day."

"Have you seen her?" Adam asked.

"No, I have not," the gentleman said. "But a friend of mine has seen her several times. And I have heard of others."

Vic walked back over to the others with his head down.

"What's the matter, buddy?" Adam asked him putting his hand on Vic's shoulder.

"Nothing," Vic said quietly not looking up.

"Vic, this man says the queen you saw walks the corridors of the palace," Adam said. Vic looked up at the gentleman.

"So, your name is Victor?" The gentleman asked. "My name is Edward." He offered his hand to Vic. "Did you know the queen you saw is named Victoria?"

Vic perked up then. Edward took Vic's book and opened it to Queen Victoria's page.

"There she is," Vic said pointing to her picture.

"Yes, that is she," Edward said. "She was a very important woman in British history."

"She smiled and waved to me," Vic said. Edward smiled as he closed the book and gave it back.

"You are a very lucky boy," Edward said. "She didn't smile or wave at many people. You are very lucky indeed."

The group went back to the hotel, had lunch and drove out to Amesbury to see Stonehenge. They were all amazed at the stone formation. Hal thought it was kind of weird about the rocks and wondered if it was an old castle from thousands of years ago, but couldn't figure how such huge stones could have been moved there.

They walked around the quaint village nearby and had some supper before going back to the hotel. Everyone packed up so they could be ready to head to the airport early in the morning. Adam set up the laptop to check the easiest route to the airport and sent an email to Ava. He received one back from her right away wishing them a safe trip and saying she will talk to him soon. Adam closed the computer and went to bed.

They got to the airport with time to spare. They went through security with no problems and checked in at the counter to get their boarding passes before finding a place to sit and wait.

"Excuse me, ma'am," Adam said. "Are you sure these are the right seats?"

"Yes, sir," the agent said showing Adam that he was in seat 4-C, Vic was in 4-D, Sally was in 4-B and Hal had 4-A. "Is there a problem with the arrangement?"

"I didn't think we were up this far in front," Adam said taking the tickets from her.

"Sir, first class only has six rows," she told him quite rudely.

"We're in first class again," Adam whispered to Hal and Sally when he sat down.

"How did that happen?" Hal asked. Adam shook his head.

"I don't know, but I'm not going to argue with anyone about it," Adam said as he sat back and kept his mouth shut about it.

Chapter 10

When they were coming in for a landing at Baldwin Regional Airport in Quincy, Adam never felt so good to be home. It was a great trip, he was glad he went, but he was glad to be home. They loaded their bags in the car and took the Plainville blacktop over to Payson and were home in a matter of twenty minutes.

"Oh, my house looks so good," Sally said as she looked for her house keys.

"It sure does," Adam said as he pulled into her driveway.

Vic jumped out and pulled out their bags. Adam got back into the car to take Hal up the street. It didn't take him long and he was walking back down the street ready to head to his apartment.

He had barely emptied his bag and put a few things away when he heard a knock at his door.

"Adam, I got your mail," Vic called.

"Thanks, buddy," Adam said as he took the mail from the boy. "You must have run both ways." Vic nodded.

"I gotta go now," Vic said as he headed for the door. Then he stopped. "Thanks for taking me, Adam. It was the best time of my life," Vic said as he hugged Adam before turning to go out the door and run down the stairs.

"You're welcome, Vic," Adam called after him then closing the door.

Adam looked through the mail and saw that they had mailed his check. He looked at the clock and knew he had about ten minutes to get to the bank. He grabbed his jacket and ran out the door and across the yard. He just made it. He knocked on Sally's door and Vic answered.

"Where's your mom?" Adam asked.

"I'm in the kitchen, come on in," Sally called. Adam walked on out to the kitchen.

"I just came from the bank," he said as he laid his rent on the table.

"Adam, that could have waited," Sally said surprised that he paid his rent already and they had only been home less than half an hour.

"Well, the bank is going to be closed tomorrow for the holiday and won't open again until Monday. I needed money anyway," he said. "Now, I am going to go upstairs and crash for a couple days." Sally laughed.

"I wish I could," she said. "I have laundry to do. If you want to throw yours down, I'll throw it in with ours."

"That's a deal," Adam said. "I'll give it to Vic."

And that's exactly what he did, too. After Vic took Adam's small bag of laundry downstairs, Adam crawled into his own bed and fell asleep. He wasn't awaken until the next day when Ava called.

"Did I wake you?" Ava asked when she heard Adam's sleepy voice.

"What was your first clue?" He grumbled at her.

"Are we getting together this weekend?" Ava asked.

"Yeah," Adam replied getting his bearings. "You want to come over here?

"Sure," Ava said. "Do you have room for me?"

"I'll make room," Adam said.

"OK," Ava said. "I'll be there around 3:00."

"Sounds good," Adam said as he looked at his clock. It was already 11:00. He could get another hour or so of sleep. So he rolled over and went back to sleep.

Adam was dreaming about the beautiful woman again. They were lying on a blanket in a park. They looked as though they were in love. He still couldn't see her face, but he knew she was very pretty with her long blond hair. He was running his fingers through her hair. He was leaning in to kiss her…

"Adam," Ava yelled as she pounded on Adam's door for the second time. "Adam, are you home?"

Adam rolled over and looked at his clock. It was 3:15.

"Holy cow," he cried as he jumped out of bed and grabbed his jeans. Ava was ready to pound one more time when she saw him walking through the kitchen.

"You just now getting up?" Ava asked as she walked in putting her bag on the sofa as Adam walked back into the bedroom not saying a word. "Nice to see you, too."

Adam walked back into the kitchen pulling on his shirt. "Sorry, jet lag," he said as he gave his sister a hug. "I think I'm back on Payson time now."

Adam looked out the window and saw Ava's car.

"What are you looking at?" Ava asked as Adam sat down at the kitchen table buttoning his shirt.

"I was just wondered if you had a driver with you," Adam teased his younger sister. She didn't think that was too funny.

"Don't be a smart ass, Adam," Ava said as she pulled out a chair and sat down. "I told Mom I was leaving and she said OK. I'm old enough to go where I want to go."

"Did you tell her where you were going?" Adam asked.

"I told her I was going to Payson," Ava said. "Whether she connected Payson with you, I don't know. She didn't say anything one way or the other."

"Did you tell anyone else?" Adam asked.

"I don't have to report to anyone, Adam," Ava said a bit disgusted. "What are you getting at?" Ava got up, walked to the refrigerator and looked inside. "You don't have anything to drink?"

"I've been gone for a week," Adam said. "And, I'm not getting at anything. I just wondered if anyone said anything about you coming over here." Adam changed the subject. "You want to go into Quincy and get something to eat? I'm starving."

"Adam, I love this place," Ava said when they walked into the Abbey.

"They have got great food here, too," Adam said pointing out their awesome nachos and super chicken wings.

"Do you just want to get appetizers…oops, I mean Abbeytizers?" Ava asked laughing at the name.

"You get enough that it's a meal," Adam said. "But you get whatever you want."

"So how's school?" Adam asked while they were waiting for their food.

"It's OK," Ava said very unconvincingly. "OK, I hate it!"

"You do? Why?" Adam was so surprised. "I thought you were happy at Truman."

"It'll probably be better next semester," Ava said. "I don't have quite as big a load as I did last semester. And I'll be taking two history classes so at least something will be interesting."

"You would have loved England," Adam said. "We walked in history. Those buildings over there are over a thousand years old. Oh, and while we were at Buckingham Palace, my landlady's son saw Queen Victoria's ghost." Ava's mouth dropped open.

"No lie?" She cried.

"No lie," Adam said. "You'll meet him. His name is Vic. But anyway, he's a special kid and he sees ghosts. He said she waved and smiled at him. Oh and you should have seen him trying to make a Beefeater crack a smile. It was too comical." Adam was laughing when he told Ava about when Vic wiggled his butt and then farted in front of the palace guard. She started laughing so hard that people around them started staring. Adam looked around and noticed people staring. He wiped his eyes and said to the closest table, "You had to have been there." They smiled at him and turned back to their food.

Adam drove around town so they could see some of the Christmas lights. Then he remembered that Quincy had one of the best Christmas Light drive thru parks in the Midwest.

"I heard about that, too," Ava said. "I saw the sign when I came through town. It was out by that big grocery store where I turned to come to your house." Adam was thinking.

"Yeah, that was 36th street. It's out at the big park on north 36th," he said. "I think tonight is the last night, too. You want to go?" Ava nodded her head."

Once Adam got close to the park the sky was illuminated above the trees with the "Avenue of Lights" sign. He and Ava were both excited and somewhat giddy with anticipation. There weren't too many cars in front of them and they were so far behind the tail lights looked like Christmas lights. Once they made the curve on the park road, they entered the world of Christmas animation.

"Oh my," Ava cooed looking from side to side. "Slow down, Adam," she cried even though he was almost at a standstill.

"Look at the snowman," Adam pointed to the left. "Oh, see the deer!" He pointed up ahead by a clump of trees.

"Look at the water wheel moving," Ava cried. "It looks like real water flowing!"

Then they went under the snowflake tunnel.

"This is so cool," Adam said getting chills.

When they exited the snowflake tunnel the small lake was on their right and the Victorian mansion was on its bank with the lights reflecting in the water. The riverboat was floating on the lake.

"Look at Cinderella's Fairy Godmother," Ava squealed. "Oh my gosh, she just changed that pumpkin into a carriage! And now the mice are horses…oh Adam, that is too cool," Ava was so excited.

They went through another tunnel of lights, saw Santa playing golf, an erupting volcano and a baby dinosaur hatching from an egg to name just a few. By the time they were coming out of the park Ava's throat was sore from squealing and Adam had a headache from the same.

"Damn, I wished I would have brought Vic," Adam said. "He would have loved this."

"Can you bring him tomorrow night?" Ava asked with a hoarse voice.

"Tonight is the last night," Adam said. "He would have gotten such a kick out of it."

"What are you doing?" Ava asked when Adam pulled into the mall parking lot.

"Sally, what are you guys doing right now?" Adam said into his phone.

"Just sitting around watching TV," Sally said. "Why are you asking?"

"Have you ever been through the Avenue of Lights?" Adam asked her.

"I took Vic through it when he was little," Sally said.

"You want to bring him in tonight? My sister and I just went through it," Adam said. "It is so amazing!"

"Vic's in the tub, Adam," Sally said. "Let's plan on it for next year, OK.

"Sure, I just thought he would love it," Adam said a little disappointed.

"Oh, I'm sure he would," Sally said. "Thanks for thinking about him."

Adam closed his phone and told Ava what Sally said.

"We'll do it next year," Adam said. "Wonder if I'll be here next year."

"What's that supposed to mean?" Ava growled at her brother.

"You never know," Adam said. "I might hit the big time and be living in Daytona." He smiled at Ava and patted her knee. She smiled.

Adam, Ava and Sally were sitting at the table after supper on Saturday when Vic came running in carrying the laptop all excited.

"I got a email from her," he cried as he set the laptop down in front of Adam.

"You got a girlfriend you ain't telling me about, boy" Adam teased as Vic opened the laptop and pulled up his email program.

"No, Adam, you silly," Vic said working very seriously to find the email. He pulled a chair up to the table and sat down. A minute or so later he found it. "There it is." The email from Regan Kislingbury opened.

"I wrote to her and she answered me," Vic said with a smile. Then he read it. "I was very pleased to receive your note. I miss you, too. It is a shame you did not get the Beefeater to laugh at you. I can imagine you were quite…Adam, what's this word?" Vic pointed to the screen.

"Comical…it means funny," Adam said.

"Comical," Vic continued. "I know I would have laughed at you. You say you saw Queen Victoria at the Palace? How…Adam, here's another one," Vic said pointing.

"Glorious…it means wonderful," Adam said.

"Glorious," Vic smiled before continuing. "It was glorious, too. How glorious it must have been for you! You must be a special person for her to wave to you." Vic paused. "You know that's what that Edward guy said, too." Sally and Adam nodded.

"Please give my regards to your family and stay in touch. Your friend in England, Regan. What does that mean?" Vic asked pointing to the last part he read.

"She wants you to say hi to us and to write her back," Adam said. Vic scratched his head.

"She sure writes funny," he said. "But she isn't American is she?"

"That was a very nice note," Sally said. "What did you write to her?"

"I told her where we went and what we saw," Vic said. "I told her what I did to the Beefeater." Vic laughed.

"What did you do to the Beefeater?" Ava asked, although she already knew. Adam shook his head and tried to keep from laughing as Vic stood up, started making faces and then burped.

"Oh my goodness," Ava said.

"That is nothing," Adam said. Vic turned around, shook his butt and was tensing up to cut one when Sally yelled at him.

"Victor, that's enough," Sally cried. Vic sat down and laughed. Adam turned his head to hide his smiles.

"He didn't," Ava asked looking at the back of Adam's head.

"He did," Sally said at which time Adam and Vic both burst out laughing.

"And the Beefeater didn't crack even a smile?" Ava asked. Adam and Vic shook their heads.

"Didn't crack a smile, not even a sparkle in his eye," Sally said.

"I bet that was funny," Ava said laughing a bit then, too, even though she had already heard the story.

"I really like Sally and Vic," Ava said when she and Adam were alone in his apartment. "She doesn't seem that much older than you."

"Don't start with me, Ava," Adam said. "We're just good friends."

"But you and Vic get along so well," Ava said.

"So," Adam said looking back at his sister.

"Well, I just thought," Ava said.

"That's the trouble with everybody," Adam said. "They think too much. Why does everybody think that everybody has to be hooked up with somebody else? Why can't a guy just be friends with a woman? We're just friends," Adam said pointing to Ava.

"I'm your sister!" Ava cried smacking Adam on the shoulder.

"But we're still friends," Adam said. Ava nodded. "That's the way I feel about Sally. I would no sooner think about taking her to bed than I would you."

"Eww, gross," Ava cried pushing Adam away from her.

"Exactly," Adam said. "But I love you. I love you very much and would do anything for you…except that." Ava smiled.

"I love you, too big brother," she said as she hugged Adam. "I just wish you could find someone to love the other way, too."

"I will, Ava," Adam said. "But I'm not ready yet. I want to get this car on the track and see what that brings. That car will be my lover." Adam turned to Ava. "Maybe tomorrow we can go up and Hal will show her to you. She is so beautiful. I can't wait to hear the engine. Feel the power under me."

"You're getting turned on talking about a piece of machinery," Ava said. Adam smiled.

"Not the way you're thinking," Adam smiled. "But yeah, it does turn me on. And you know when I'm in a car feeling the heat from the engine, feeling the roar of the engine, the power…I know I am in control of a monstrous machine. It gives me a feeling like no other. I get into my own world and just go."

Ava was watching her brother enter a different world. His eyes were looking into a far off place. His body was reacting to something that wasn't in the room. He leaned one way and then the other. His hands were holding on to an imaginary wheel and he was steering. Although he was standing his feet were controlling the pedals and he was driving a winning car.

Ava pretended she had a flag in her hand and waved it up and down.

"And Adam Dieker gets the checkered flag!" Ava cried bringing Adam out of his trance.

"Ava it is like nothing I can explain," Adam said with beads of sweat on his brow.

"You were in the zone just then," Ava said. "You were there"

"That's why I can't have a woman right now," Adam said. "There's no room for her. I need and want to give 100% to this car. I want it to be the best she can be so we can take her to the limit. I don't want to stay on these small tracks for the rest of my life. I'd like to have my name up there with Gordon, Earnhardt and all the other big guys someday."

"I'd say you're on your way with this attitude," Ava said.

"And Hal has got some good guys coming to work on her," Adam said excitedly. "And now he has some good sponsors. So now all he needs is my full attention and 100% effort put into the team. We can do it."

Sunday after lunch Hal, Ava and Adam walked out to garage to see the car. The sun was shining brightly on the cold winter day and as the door opened, the light reflected off the chrome of the engine as if a million watt spotlight had been flashed in their eyes. Ava put her hand up to shade the glare and she saw the car.

"Wow, she is a beauty," Ava said walking over to the car. "Do you come out and dust her off every day?" She teased Hal.

"No, that's Adam's job," Hal teased back. Ava walked around the car and just stared.

"Unbelievable," Ava said.

"She don't understand us, does she boy?" Hal said. Adam shook his head and smiled.

When they got back to Hal's house they had missed a call, but there was a message for Hal.

"This is Randy Conners. Give me a call." Hal was ecstatic! He quickly called Randy back.

The call was very brief and Hal had the biggest smile on his face when he hung up the phone.

"Boy, you want to start working on the car this coming week?" Hal asked Adam.

"You serious?" Adam replied with a question.

"That was Randy and he will be here on Wednesday," Hal said.

"I've been waiting for this for so long," Adam said hugging Hal.

"You been waiting for so long?" Hal said. "How the hell long you think I been waiting?"

"I guess that means my visit is over," Ava said although she was happy for the guys.

"Sorry, baby sister, but unless you want to sit around and watch," Adam said.

"No, that's OK," Ava said. "I was planning on leaving tomorrow anyway since you have to go back to work."

"Oh yea," Adam said. "I do have to go back to work, don't I?" He started laughing.

Chapter 11

Adam couldn't wait for 4:30 to come on Wednesday afternoon. It had snowed that morning and kids were dragging slush all over the place. He would get once area cleaned up and find it a mess when he walked back through a half hour later. He figured he would get the classrooms finished and lock them up then give the halls one last run before locking the building for the night. He was in a hurry to get over to Hal's place.

The garage was closed and Hal and Randy were in the house. They were sitting at the kitchen table talking over coffee.

"Ah, here's my boy now," Hal said when Adam walked in the house.

Hal introduced Randy to Adam. Randy was built about the same as Adam but about two inches shorter. He knew his way around engines and could put one together in the dark. Hal had every confidence that Randy was the best choice for chief mechanic.

"So what do you think of that beauty out there?" Adam asked Randy as he pulled out a chair and sat down running his hand through his hair.

"Looks pretty sweet to me," Randy said. "I think I know where we can get new parts for her and once we get that tweaked, she ought to fly."

"Will you have trouble finding them for her?" Hal asked.

"Not really," Randy said taking a sip of his coffee.

"So when are you going to start working on her?" Adam asked not hiding his excitement.

"We're moving her into Willie's big garage across the street. We'll have lots of room and it's wired for all of our equipment," Hal said. "Bobby said he would even rig up a hoist for us."

"Is Bobby working with us?" Adam asked. Hal nodded.

"Yea," Hal said. "So far, I have Bobby, Dusty and Eddie helping us out. And Colin said he's coming the first of next week. I don't know if he's staying the whole season though."

"Don't forget to count me in," Adam said.

"You can watch and hand us tools," Randy said. "But you won't be doing much more than shining the fenders." Adam looked disappointed. "Sorry, kid. Your job is to drive her to victory. Mine is to make sure she's in the best possible mechanical condition for you."

"I suppose so," Adam said.

"Don't look so sad," Randy said. You're the only one who's going to get to drive her. I do all the work and can't even take her for a spin. Doesn't seem fair, does it?"

"Never thought about it like that," Adam said smiling.

Adam picked up Colin at the Quincy airport the following week and filled him on what they had done so far. Colin was going to stay with Hal while he was in Payson and decide if he was staying for the entire season. Colin loved the scenery on the way from the airport to Payson.

Colin and Randy hit it off right away. They worked together so well that Hal didn't worry about a thing. Instead of arguing like some American teams would do, Colin and Randy discussed possibilities and tried one and if it didn't work simply tried something else. Adam and Hal both thought it was a pleasure working with them.

Colin and Randy worked mostly in the afternoon and evening when they were joined for a few hours by Bobby, Dusty and Eddie who all had other jobs. And of course, young Vic was there every day running for this or that and helped out with anything he could.

One Friday afternoon in mid March Adam walked over to the garage and no one was working. The hood on the car was down, too. He quickly walked over to Hal's to find Colin, Randy, Vic and Hal sitting around the table.

"About time you got home," Hal grumbled as he got up and started for the door.

"You know I work until 4:30," Adam snapped back at Hal following him out the door.

The entire group of men walked over to the garage. Adam just figured he interrupted their break. But when they got inside the garage Colin ordered Adam to climb in behind the wheel. Adam looked stunned.

"Well, get in," Colin ordered Adam.

Adam climbed in. He felt good sitting in the car.

“You look good in there,” Hal called as Adam ran his hand through his hair.

“Feels good,” Adam said smiling from ear to ear.

“Turn her on,” Randy called through the window.

Adam was so excited his hand was shaking. This was the first time he was going to feel the power of the car under his body. Oh, sure, he had heard the engine while they were working on it, but he was going to feel it now. He reached down, turned the ignition and gave it some gas. The engine fired up! Adam felt the purr of the motor. He smiled.

“Give her some fuel,” Colin ordered. Adam nodded.

Adam pressed and released the accelerator and the monster roared! Adam felt the chills run through his body. He felt the adrenaline pumping. He pressed it again and the car roared louder. Adam closed his eyes for just a second imagining himself on the track. He couldn’t wait.

Randy gave the cut signal and Adam turned off the car. He didn’t want to get out right away. Colin stuck his head in the window.

“What do you think of her?” He asked Adam as Adam had a smile stuck on his face.

“Sweet,” Adam said stretching the word out as far as he could.

Colin pulled his head out of the window and looked over to Randy and Hal.

“I think he likes her,” Colin said smiling.

Saturday morning Bobby came with the trailer and loaded up the car to take it to the race track for a test run. Adam was more excited than Vic. Hal thought he had two little boys on his hands.

“Are you always like this on race days?” Hal asked Adam teasing him.

“No,” Adam said. “I never felt like this before.”

“You’re acting like a virgin groom on his wedding night,” Randy teased him.

All the way to the race track the guys were teasing Adam something fierce. He was so glad when they pulled in and he could get out to help roll the car into the garage area.

Adam took the car for its first test run on the quarter mile track. She purred like a kitten. He felt the power under his body wanting to be unleashed but he didn’t want to put her full out just yet. He went around the track a couple times letting her build speed. With each pass of the starter's block the bleachers became blurred. The new blooms of the red bud trees amidst the white of the dogwoods and green of the new budding maples and oaks in the woods at turns three and four blurred as if it was a small child's finger painting. He no longer saw individual people standing on pit road as he whizzed by. He went faster and faster.

"Bring her in, Adam," Hal ordered through Adam's ear piece on his fifth lap. Adam's adrenaline was pumping and he didn't want to obey his boss, but he slowed the car down and drove it down into pit road coming to a stop in front of the crew.

"How'd she do?" Hal asked the young man as he pulled himself out of the car. Adam pulled off his helmet and leaned against the car as if caressing a lover.

"She wants to run," Adam said rubbing the top of the car as if he was stroking a beautiful woman. "I could feel her wanting to go, but I didn't want to push too much today being it was our first time together."

"Know what she did?" Hal asked. Adam shook his head. "Clocked her at 96."

Adam whistled. "I wasn't even pushing her either. She drifted around the curves so smooth."

"So you think she could do more than that?" Hal asked as he sat on the pit wall looking at the beautiful black machine.

"Definitely," Adams said. "I felt like I was cruising down Highway 36 on a Sunday afternoon."

"Yee ha," Hal yelled slapping his thigh.

"When's the first race?" Adam asked anxious to get out among a pack of contenders.

"Not real sure," Hal said. "It's usually around the middle of April though."

Instead of taking the car back to the Willie's garage, Bobby took it over to the body shop in town. They had the detail paint plan for the car and were going to work on that this week. Hal, Adam and Vic were looking at the image that Brett had on the computer to give their final approval before anything was done.

There was going to be a white 26 trimmed in yellow and green on both doors and on top. They were going to have KISCO across the front in bright yellow trimmed in green. Adam really didn't like those colors, but it was KISCO's color scheme and they were a major sponsor. On the trunk were the golden arches from McDonald's. Vic went in to the McDonald's manager one day when they were having lunch. He simply asked if he wanted to sponsor his friend's stock car. Next thing they knew, Adam had a major sponsor. Adam's name was written in white script across the back on both sides and Wavering Lawn Care on both sides of the front in their yellow and green.

Brett turned the 3D image so they could see it from all angles. It did look pretty sharp. Adam really liked the way his name was going to look on the sides.... Adam Dieker.

"They'll know it's me when they see that," Adam said pointing to his name.

"I really like that, too," Brett said. "It looks classy."

"That us," Hal said. "We're totally classy."

"We'll have it done by Friday," Brett said.

"Give us a call," Hal said as he, Vic and Adam walked out.

Friday afternoon Adam was walking over to the bank when he saw the trailer at the garage. He slipped into the bank real quick and when he walked out he saw Vic standing outside of the garage waving like a mad man. He was yelling but Adam couldn't make it out. Adam didn't stop at his place and just walked straight up to the garage.

"Close your eyes," Vic ordered reaching up to Adam's eyes.

"Don't be silly, Vic," Adam said pushing the boy's hand down.

"Listen to the boy," Hal barked meeting them at the door. "Close your eyes." Adam did as he was told and Hal and Vic led him in.

"OK," Vic giggled. "Open them up!"

Adam opened his eyes and saw the shiny black car completely detailed. He squealed like a teen age girl.

"Oh my gosh!" Adam cried as he walked around and ran his hand through his hair. Tears were coming to his eyes. "Oh my gosh! She's beautiful! She's so beautiful!" Adam walked up to the car and touched the roof and ran his hand gently across the top.

"You like her?" Vic asked. Adam put his arm around Vic's shoulders. He nodded.

"Yeah, little man, I like her," Adam said. "I like her a lot." Then, looking down at Vic, Adam asked, "Do you like her?"

"I love her," Vic said. "I think she's a winner."

"From your mouth to God's ears," Hal said.

Chapter 12

Adam was tired. He had worked all day at school and they had been working on the car for the last two hours. He needed a break. Adam walked out of the garage toward pit road. The western sky was still bright streaked with red, orange and yellow. The sun was hidden behind some puffy clouds that no longer appeared white as they had less than a half hour earlier. Adam sat on the wall along the pit. He was excited about the race coming up soon, too, and knew the car was in good shape.

Adam loved the smells of the racetrack, the freshly disturbed dirt, the oils and gases. The mixtures of all the new life blooming in the woods around the racetrack filled the air. Adam could smell the dogwood, the redbud and the wild honeysuckle. Adam turned away from the sunset and looked toward the woods. He couldn't see the colors of the trees right now. But what he did see disturbed him.

There was a woman walking on the track down by curve four. What was she doing there? He couldn't make her out very well so he got up and walked toward her. She wore a long dark skirt and white long sleeve blouse. She had long blonde hair that was blowing behind her. Adam thought that was strange since there was very little breeze.

"Adam," Vic yelled from the edge of the drive to the garages. "Adam, you out here?"

Adam turned around when Vic called him. He turned back to take another look at the woman but she was gone. Adam thought that was very strange.

"Maybe I'm just over tired," Adam said to himself as he started back toward Vic. "I'm here." He called out to the young boy.

The image of the woman stuck in Adam's mind on their ride back to Payson. Hal was pretty quiet in the passenger's seat and by the time they hit their turn off Adam heard Hal's gentle snores.

"You saw her, huh," Vic said quietly from the back seat.

"What?" Adam said as if he didn't hear the boy's comment.

"You saw the lady on turn four tonight," Vic repeated adding a little more to his statement.

"I think I saw something," Adam said softly. "Who is she?"

"They say I'm silly 'cause I see her," Vic said, not answering Adam's question. Vic didn't say anymore for the rest of the trip home.

Adam thought that if Vic saw her and he, himself, could see her then she had to be real. But who is she and what was she doing so late out on the track all alone? He wished he could get closer to her, and maybe even talk to her. He would also like to talk to Vic about her more. But, he didn't think he should mention anything to Sally or Hal yet, since they say that Vic is silly since he sees her and they can't. He wondered why they couldn't see her or was she someone that they didn't want to talk about with Vic. Adam's mind was jumbled with so many ideas about this woman he only saw for a few moments. Yet she seemed so familiar.

The next day at school Adam talked to a few of the racing fans as he always did at lunch time. They asked Adam how far Hal's car was coming along and if he thought it was going to be ready for the first race. Adam was just getting ready to fill them in on the details when Steve Maynard set his lunch tray down at the table.

"So you saw her," Steve said as he moved some of the other seniors so he could sit down across from Adam. "Vic told me."

"I did," Adam said looking the biggest kid at the table in the eye. "Who is she?"

"You don't want to know," Steve said. "And you don't want to race at Mill Creek."

"What?" Adam cried then laughed at the warning. "You can't tell me not to race because I saw a woman on the track. And, you won't tell me anything about her." Adam started to get up from the table.

Steve reached over and put his hand on Adam's arm to keep him from leaving.

"She's warning you," Steve said. The other boys at the table had very serious looks on their faces and glanced from Steve to Adam as if they were watching a tennis match. They all knew the story and wondered if Steve was going to tell all. But it wasn't going to happen just now. The bell signaling the end of lunch rang and all the students rushed out of the cafeteria.

"She's warning you," Steve repeated before he picked up his tray and walked out.

Adam slowly picked up his tray, dumped his trash and put his tray in the window. He watched as the last of the students left before starting to pick up the tables to clean the floors.

All afternoon, Adam thought about Steve's warning. Who could he talk to about this? Should he find the students after school and talk to them? Should he mention it to Hal? Would Hal laugh at him or lie since he wanted a winning driver? Would young Vic be the one to talk to? No matter what, Adam had to find out.

Later that afternoon Adam was walking toward the office to vacuum the carpet when he walked by the school library. Maybe the library would have some information. He pushed on the door and it was still open. Kelly Fanning, the librarian, was still there.

"Hey Kelly," Adam said walking over to the counter to talk to her.

"Hi Adam, are you looking for a book to read?" Kelly asked him. Kelly had lived in the area all her life, was single and thought Adam was quite handsome. Her cousin had been a top racer at Mill Creek a few years ago, so Adam was hoping she could help him if there were no books on the subject.

"Kelly, I was wondering if you have any books here about Mill Creek," Adam asked her.

Kelly was kind of disappointed he was actually looking for books, but she was happy to help.

"You talking about the race track?" Kelly asked him as she got up and walked around the counter.

"Yeah," Adam replied stepping back allowing her to walk into the main part of the library.

"I think there are some magazines and we have newspaper article archives on the computer now," Kelly told him leading him over to the periodical section. "Is there anything special you are looking for?"

Adam was kind of nervous bringing up the woman to Kelly.

"Are there any superstitions about the track?" Adam asked her. "You know, since I am going to be driving out there, I'd like to know about them."

"What have you heard?" Kelly turned around and sat on the edge of a table. Her whole demeanor changed and she didn't seem as willing to help now.

"Nothing," Adam said which was true. "I just like to check out a track before I race on it."

Kelly looked at Adam. She walked back towards the counter not saying anything.

"You can't help me?" Adam asked her. Kelly turned around when she reached the counter looking straight into his brown eyes.

"There is a story," Kelly said. "I don't know if you call it a superstition, though. I don't have time to tell it to you now and you probably have work to finish."

"Let me take you to dinner one evening and you can tell me all about it," Adam suggested.

"What night doesn't Hal have you out at the track working on the car?" Kelly asked.

"He lets me have a night off now and then," Adam said. "Tell me when you want to go and I'll tell him I am busy that night."

"What about tomorrow night?" Kelly suggested they go to the Abbey after school. "We can go early and get half price appetizers. I'll tell you all about it then."

Adam finished work quickly, ran home to shower and change clothes before Kelly was to pick him up around 4:45. He saw her car pull up down by the garage, stuffed his wallet in his pocket and pulled on a light jacket before running down the stairs. When he got to the car, Kelly had slid over to the passenger side. The window was down.

"You wanna drive?" She called to him. Adam nodded as he went around the car and got in.

When Adam and Kelly walked into the Abbey he noticed she was carrying a rather large file. He hoped she brought articles about the race track for him.

When the hostess walked over to them Kelly said something to her and they were led to the east side of the place where it was very bright and much quieter. Once they were seated, had ordered drinks and looked over the menus, Kelly put the folder on the table. She folded her hands on top of it.

"So, you want to know the story about the race track," Kelly said looking over at Adam. "Who told you there was a story?"

Adam didn't know whether he should tell her everything or just tell her enough to get her talking.

"Well, I've heard things," Adam said looking Kelly straight in her deep blue eyes. His daddy always told him if you look someone in the eye they're more likely to believe you.

"Several years ago, Scott had powder puff racing for a while. The fans loved it and there were enough women to make it work." Kelly continued telling the story.

"During the summer Scott set aside Wednesday nights for the girls. He had two divisions and the crowds grew. He was very happy with the way things were turning out. There were some drivers coming from as far as Donnellson and Decatur and some of them were getting big name sponsors. Most of the men didn't mind sharing the track with the women as long as they didn't share the same night with them. Oh, there were a few hot heads that caused a little trouble, but Scott told them not to come back if they didn't like the way he was running things."

"One of them was a Danny something from Mt. Pleasant. He thought he was a big tough guy and was a nasty driver so a lot of the guys were glad to see him go. He came down to watch the girls' race and see how much trouble he could cause as a spectator. He never crossed the line to where he would get ejected from the track, though. Or at least he never got caught, until that day."

"The last night of powder puff, Danny was in the infield between turns three and four. He was so liquored up he could barely walk. About half way into the feature one of the cars slid up into two of the other cars between the curves. One of the cars was pushed hard into the wall and the other skidded along it. It was real bad. One girl died and one girl is still in pretty bad shape."

"The girl that skidded into the other cars said Danny was flashing the cars. It broke her concentration for just a split second causing her to hit the other cars." Kelly paused to take a sip of her tea.

"You mean he…" Adam asked as he felt his cheeks blush.

"Yeah," Kelly said as she continued. "Another driver backed up her story; and Danny is in prison for involuntary man slaughter. He tried to fight it, but didn't do any good. Danny has been spending most of his time in solitary for his own protection because so many of the prisoners are race fans and when they heard what he did, they wanted to seek revenge."

Adam sat dumbfounded listening to such a horrifying story. So, the woman he saw, was she the driver that died? Dare he ask Kelly about that? Their food had arrived and he wanted to give her time to eat. It was then that Kelly slid the folder to Adam.

"You can glance through this while we eat," she said. "And I'll finish the story when we are done. And I can answer any questions you have then." Adam nodded. Did he look like he had questions?

Adam opened the folder to find newspaper clippings…many newspaper clippings. There were pictures of the wrecked cars, a mug shot picture of Danny along side of his racing photo. There were racing photos of the three drivers involved in the accident…one was just as pretty as the other. There was the obituary of the driver that was killed. It was quite long giving detailed information as to how the accident happened and the injuries she sustained. Her name was Shari Rose Fanning. Adam stopped reading and looked up. He pointed to what he was reading and Kelly nodded. The driver was Kelly's sister.

"I am so sorry," Adam said. "If I had known…"

"It's all right," Kelly said. "She needs to be remembered."

Adam really wondered if he should mention the fact that he saw her now.

"You know, there's a rumor that says she walks the racetrack," Kelly said looking over at Adam.

"Oh really?" Adam said trying to sound surprised and very interested.

"They wanted to have someone from T.A.P.S. come and check it out, but it's hard to get someone that big to come out here," Kelly said.

"You talking about that ghost hunters group from Rhode Island?" Adam said.

"They are a paranormal group, yes," Kelly said. "Anyway, some people say they have seen her. Stories have been made up that she is looking for a love to carry her into the next world."

"That's romantic," Adam said with a little giggle.

"It's kept a lot of guys from driving here," Kelly said. "There was one driver that said he saw her the night before a race when he was out testing the car. She was standing on the track by the fourth curve. He said she was just standing there and it startled him. He wasn't going that fast that he missed hitting her. When he told his crew they all laughed at him and said he needed a good night sleep. The next day at the race, his car started giving him some trouble on the first lap around the fourth curve. He took it into the pit and got it taken care of and went right back out. He was doing great and catching up close to the leader. There was no one even close to him when he hit the wall on the fourth turn. It ended his racing career. When they asked him what happen, he said his car just shut down."

Adam wondered if that is what Steve was warning him about. Kelly still had more to tell.

"That's not the only time that has happened," Kelly continued. "There were three other drivers over the years that said they had seen her. Each time during their feature, they had accidents on her curve. Only one of the three continued to race after his accident. But he refuses to come back to Mill Creek."

Adam looked at the newspaper clippings. He was looking for a date. He looked up at Kelly. This would be the fifth summer racing season since Shari Rose's death. Adam would be the fifth racer that has seen her spirit. Should he tell her that he has seen Shari Rose?

"Adam, is all this talk about spirits scaring you?" Kelly asked the strong young man sitting across from her holding the picture of a beautiful young woman.

Adam looked at Kelly then down at Shari Rose's picture.

"I saw her," Adam said softly to Kelly whose face dropped. "I saw her the other night after we were working on the car. She had on a long dark skirt, a light colored long sleeve blouse. Her long blonde hair was blowing behind her but there wasn't any breeze or wind at all," Adam recounted every detail as if he was still sitting on the pit wall. "I wanted to walk closer to talk to her but they called me back."

"Don't race, Adam," Kelly said. "Please don't race." Tears were coming to Kelly's eyes.

"You know young Vic," Adam said. "He says he sees her. We didn't get to talk much because there were other people around. But, he says people told him he is silly. But he says he sees her."

"You can't believe the boy," Kelly said. "You know how he is."

"But, Kelly," Adam started. "I think I believe him about this. He knew I had seen her. Why would he bring her up? Come home with me and let's talk to him."

"Well, I'm not sure Sally would want us to talk to him about it," Kelly said trying to talk Adam out of getting Vic involved.

"Let's call her first," Adam said pulling out his phone. Kelly nodded her but put her hand on Adam's hand asking him to allow her to call Sally.

"Sally, Adam and I want to talk to Vic about Shari Rose," Kelly said waiting to hear Sally's reply.

"Kel, you know we try to discourage that," Sally said. "Why does Adam want to know about that?"

"He's seen her," Kelly said. There was nothing from the other end. "Sally, you there?"

"My God, Kel, not Adam," Sally said. Kelly could tell that Sally was on the verge of tears.

"Yeah," Kelly said. Sally told Kelly to come on out and they could talk to Vic.

"Hey buddy," Adam said when he and Kelly walked into Sally's house. Vic gave Kelly a hug and a high five to Adam.

"You go on a date with her?" Vic whispered to Adam smiling.

"No, pal, we just had supper together," Adam told him. "You know who my girl friend is,"

"A black beauty 350 stock car," Vic and Adam said together laughing. "And don't you ever forget it," Adam said teasingly poking Vic in the chest. Vic laughed as he fell into the big chair.

"Victor, don't plop on the furniture," Sally scolded him.

"Hey, Vic, you remember the other night when you asked me if I saw the woman at the track." Adam was sitting across from Vic wanting to have the conversation just between the two of them. Vic looked to his mother. Sally nodded.

"Yeah, I remember," Vic said. "She was there when I called you."

"Have you ever talked to her?" Adam asked hoping they would get some reason why she was there.

"I tried once," Vic said. "I said, 'Hi Shari Rose, I'm Vic.' But she just cried. I asked her why does she cry. She looked out into the timber and cried some more. She didn't talk to me."

"Did she ever run away from you," Adam asked. Vic shook his head.

"Did you ever give her anything? Or did she ever give you anything?" Adam wasn't sure what questions to ask, but he just knew he needed answers.

"I gave her a flower one time," Vic said. "I just picked it by the creek. She like it and patted me on the head." Vic put his hand on the top of his head as if remembering the moment.

Sally looked disturbed that her son was on the outside of the race way fence along the creek.

Vic jumped up and ran into his room. A matter of a few seconds he was back holding something tightly in his hand. He stood before Adam and uncurled his hand to expose a gold cross on a chain.

Kelly gasped at the sight of it. Sally put her arms around Kelly.

"One time she gave me this," Vic said. "She told me to keep it safe and to give it to my very best friend some day."

"That's a pretty special gift," Adam said. "You take good care of it." Adam put his hand around Vic's and closed the boy's hand around the jewelry. "Go put it away somewhere safe now." Vic did as he was told.

"She was wearing that the day of the race and it was never found," Kelly said. "We even thought maybe someone at the hospital might have taken it. I feel so bad now."

Vic slowly walked back into the room shuffling his feet. His head was lowered and his hands were folded. He walked over stopping in front of Adam.

"Adam, you and me's buds, right," Vic said. Adam nodded. "We's best buds I think. I think," the young lad paused looking back down at his hands.

"What are you getting to?" Adam asked the boy who looked up to Adam cocking his head.

"You know I never really had a really best friend other than my mom and she don't count," Vic looked over to Sally. "Sorry Mom, you're still my best girl friend."

"Thanks Vic," Sally said smiling at her special son.

"Anyways, Shari Rose told me to give this to my best friend," Vic said as he opened his hand exposing the cross and chain again. "She didn't say so but I think it will bring you good luck. I think you will win every race with it."

Vic stretched his hand out letting the cross dangle from the chain. Adam knew how special the cross was to the boy and how special the gift meant. Adam put his hand under the cross just letting it touch his palm to stop it from swinging back and forth. Vic lowered it slowly and when it was just about to Adam's hand, Adam enclosed the chain and cross in his and Vic's hands in a handshake. Vic thought that was so cool. He felt real special because now he and Adam had a true bond.

"Thank you, Vic," Adam said sincerely. "This means so much to me. You and I are really best buds." Vic reached over and hugged

Adam. Sally was choking back the tears seeing the smile on her son. Adam was holding back the tears knowing for the first time how wonderful such unconditional love from another human really feels.

Adam asked Kelly to come to the kitchen with him for a minute. Knowing the cross meant so much to Kelly, Adam asked her how she felt about what went down with Vic giving it to him.

"Oh my God, Adam, I couldn't be happier," Kelly said. "To see how special that little piece of gold made that boy feel…I can't tell you. If Shari Rose actually did give it to him and told him to give it to his best friend, he could not have picked a better pal. I know it will be taken care of and appreciated for what it actually is…a gift from a best friend." Kelly put the chain around Adam's neck and adjusted it.

"Thanks, Kelly," Adam said as he gave her a little hug. "I just wanted to make sure you are OK with it." Kelly kissed Adam on the cheek. Adam blushed.

"I thought you said she wasn't your girl friend," Vic said standing in the kitchen door visibly upset.

"She's not," Adam said as he walked over to Vic. "You know that I would tell my best bud if I ever had a girl friend. And you already know who my girl friend is."

"A black beauty 350 stock car," Vic and Adam said together laughing enjoying the joke.

"Don't worry, buddy. You'll be the first to know if I ever get a new girl friend," Adam said with a laugh. "And you know, she might just be a cherry red 350 late model stock." That tickled Vic and he roared with laughter until he had tears.

"I can see your babies," Vic cried through his tears of laughter. "You'll have baby hobby cars."

This got the adults laughing then. Vic could come up with some cute ones now and then. Sometimes they made no sense but he did make you laugh.

Chapter 13

It was finally race day! Adam woke up so early ready to go. It was too early to go up to Hal's. It was even too early to go downstairs to Sally's. Even though he took a shower the night before, he took another shower then sat on his bed. He grabbed his Bible and opened it and read for a few minutes before he realized he was getting cold. He put the book down and got dressed. He was just finishing brushing his hair when someone knocked at his door.

"Hey Vic," Adam said when he saw his buddy at the door.

"Mom says to come down now for breakfast," Vic said as he turned around and ran down the stairs.

"Be right there," Adam called after him.

Adam grabbed his jacket, stuffed his wallet in his pocket and ran his hand through his hair. He closed the door behind him and ran down the stairs.

Sally had fixed a nice breakfast of scrambled eggs, bacon, and muffins. She had a big pitcher of orange juice sitting in the middle of the table, too.

"Wow, this looks really good," Adam said. "Thanks so much."

"Well, we figured we needed to send you off on a full stomach," Sally said as she scooped the eggs onto Adam's plate.

Adam poured a glass of orange juice for Vic before pouring his own glass. Sally set a platter of bacon and a cozy of muffins on the table. Vic was licking is lips ready to dig in when his mom and Adam took his hands and lowered their heads.

"Let me," Vic asked. Adam and Sally nodded.

"Thank You for our food my mom made for us. And please God, keep Adam and all the racers safe today but let Adam end up at the front when it is all over. Amen."

"Amen," Sally and Adam said in unison both of them smiling.

“I sure hope God is listening,” Sally said picking up her fork.

“He’s always listening,” Adam said looking over at her. She smiled and nodded.

Adam thanked Sally for breakfast then he and Vic walked up to Hal’s. The car was already loaded on the hauler and Bobby, Dusty and Eddie were sitting in the kitchen with Hal, Colin and Randy drinking coffee and tea.

“There’s my boys,” Hal said. “Want anything to drink?”

“No thanks,” Adam said. “Sally just fixed us a nice breakfast.”

“Hope you’re not a puker,” Randy teased. Adam didn’t think he was too funny.

“How do you feel, boy?” Hal asked Adam.

“Pretty good,” Adam said. “I’m excited and ready to get out there, but I’m a little nervous, too. I always am on the first race of the season, though.”

“If you are not a bit nervous,” Colin said looking at Adam, “you are not human, I’d say.” The others agreed.

It was finally time to get everyone to their vehicles and head for the track. Vic wanted to ride with Adam, of course.

The track was abuzz with other teams getting their cars ready, going over last minute check lists. Drivers were heading to the first meeting of the season to go over rules of the track. Hal went with Adam as most owners accompanied their drivers to this meeting.

Scott welcomed the men and promised he would give them a great racing season as in years past. The rules were pretty much the same. He added that there was going to be absolutely no smoking at all around the garages inside or outside within fifty feet of any building or any race car. There was a groan from several racers. It seemed last year there was a fire caused by a cigarette near one of the cars on a trailer. If a crew member hadn’t been observant they could have lost several cars to someone’s negligence.

“Hey man, good to see you back with us,” a driver said to Adam.

“Thanks,” Adam said as he and Hal were walking back to the garage.

“Who was that?” Hal asked.

“That’s Rich Uppinghouse,” Adam said. “I used to race with him a couple years ago.”

“With him,” Hal asked.

“Well, you know what I mean,” Adam said. “We weren’t team

mates or anything." Adam saw another guy he knew. "Hey man!"

When they got back to the garage, Colin told Adam the car was ready for him to get out on the track for practice. Adam was ready. His heart was pounding. He climbed in the car and started it. The car sounded great.

"Take it slow going out to the track," Randy yelled at him over the roar of the engine. Adam nodded.

"Can you hear me, boy?" Hal spoke in a normal voice.

"Yeah, fine," Adam replied since he heard Hal through the speaker in his helmet. "Can you hear me now?" Adam giggled thinking of the cell phone commercial.

"Get serious, son," Hal ordered.

"Yes, sir," Adam said as he settled down and drove the car onto pit road. He got the signal from the pit chief and headed onto the track. He took a run around and gradually picked up speed. The track felt real good…better than it had the other night. There was no one around him so he swerved a bit on the straight away to feel out the steering. Everything felt really good.

"Bring her in," Colin ordered. Adam brought the car down pit road and stopped where he saw his crew. He stayed in the car.

"How'd she feel?" Randy asked.

"Real good," Adam said.

"Any vibrations?" Colin asked. Adam shook his head.

Eddie was filling the tank.

Adam was walking around like a caged lion waiting for his race. He knew the car was ready and he was ready. He walked over to the car and leaned up against it folding his hands on the roof. It looked to everyone else that he was looking in the window, but Adam was praying.

"Dear God, just let me do well, not make a fool out of myself, or disappoint my team," Adam said. "Amen. Oh, and please keep me and the other drivers safe, Lord."

He flattened his hands on top of the car and rubbed the roof and whispered to the car. "It's you and me, girl," he said softly.

"That fool kid is talking to that car," Randy said to Hal.

"If that's what it takes to win, let him talk," Hal said.

There were only ten cars in Adam's Heat Race and he blew his competition away leaving them so far behind, you'd think they were in another race. When they got the green flag he pulled out ahead of them, found his grove and took off. He flew down the chute, drifted around the curves and left his competition almost a whole lap behind him. Adam felt so good as he pulled into the pit.

"You made that look so easy," Randy said patting Adam on the back as he climbed out of the car pulling off his helmet.

"It felt easy," Adam said running his hand across the roof of the car then pushing his hair back off his brow.

"Car running OK, son?" Hal asked him. Adam nodded.

"I never ran one that felt so smooth," Adam said looking at the black beauty.

Adam had a several minutes before his next race. He went back to the garage area to go to the restroom and get something to drink. Vic wanted to go along with him. Adam put his arm around Vic's shoulders as they started walking toward the garage.

"What do you think, buddy?" Adam asked the smiling kid.

"You're a real champ," Vic said grinning from ear to ear.

"Good answer," Adam said ruffling Vic's hair.

Adam ordered Vic to wait for him while they were in the drivers' locker area. All the while Adam complained about getting out of the jump suit just to go.

"Good thing I didn't wait until the last minute," he said to Vic.

"Got that right," Vic said. "You want to use a diaper?" Vic started laughing at the joke. Sometimes Adam thought that wouldn't be such a bad idea when he was in a long race.

Adam was still complaining about the jump suit after he stepped out of the stall pulling himself back together when the racetrack's mascot, Zippy, the duck came in. He had heard Adam complaining.

"You think you got problems," Zippy said as he slipped into the large stall at the end and worked to get out of his costume so he could get his business done. Adam and Vic laughed. After thinking a moment, Adam decided he didn't have anything to complain about really.

Adam was getting antsy waiting around for his next race. Originally there were 37 cars entered but one car dropped out. He was sitting on the wall when Vic came over to tell him about the driver dropping out.

"Adam," Vic whispered as he sat down next to Adam. "They say the driver refuses to get in the car. He said he saw her."

"Who?" Adam asked the boy.

"You know," Vic said nodding toward the fourth curve.

"Today?" Adam asked. "He saw her today?" Vic nodded.

"He won't drive anymore," Vic said. "He said he won't ever come back here."

Adam looked out toward the spot he had seen Shari Rose. The only thing he saw were the trees in full spring colors being passed by the modified stock cars. He scanned the area and there was no sight of her at all.

Adam had to start at the middle of the pack of his first Feature of the season. He figured if he could pass the few cars in front of him, he could start the year off with a win and 22 solid points.

He saw the first three cars pass him in the pits to get lined up and thought that this was the last time they would be doing that. When the last one passed him, he pulled into position and they were on the track. They gained speed and the starter waved the green flag and they were off.

Adam immediately passed the first couple cars in front of him before hitting the first curve then went down low passing another one. He pulled away from the pack and just cruised around as if he were the only car out there.

On the eighth lap two cars behind him slid into the wall which brought out the yellow flag. Almost all the cars did a quick splash and go while the track was cleared of the accident. Luckily both drivers were not injured.

Rich Uppinghouse caught up with him during the caution and was going to try to draft him but Adam weaved back and forth not letting him get in tight and close. Adam also kept an eye on the starting block and as soon as he saw that flag go up in the air and then come down he put his foot down and let Rich behind.

Adam was in the lead and there were only two laps to go. He rounded turn 4 and saw the starter give him the white flag. He really felt good. He felt he had this race in his pocket. Easy around the course one more time with nobody even close and he got the checkered flag.

When he crossed the finish line and saw the flag fall he let out a war hoop so loud that Hal pulled off his head set rubbing his ear.

Adam went around the track once more being sure not to interfere with the other drivers still racing and went into the pit.

"You made that race quite exciting, my boy," Colin said as he helped Adam out of the car. Adam pulled his helmet off and pushed his hair back.

The crew was very happy with the win. Vic was jumping up and down and when he knew it was OK, ran over to Adam and jumped up into his arms.

"I knew you're a champ," Vic said. "I knew it." Adam swung the boy around laughing.

"Now that I'm deaf," Hal yelled over the roar of the crowd, "Good job, son. Very good job."

"Thanks, Hal," Adam said as hugged his boss lifting the old man off his feet. Colin, Randy, Bobby and Eddie laughed when Hal protested and told Adam to put him down.

"You kiss me and we're through," Hal cried when Adam put him down getting more laughs from the crew.

"Old man," Adam started. "I'm going to give you the biggest kiss you ever got when we win the championship."

"I'll hold you to that one, boy" Hal said. "I'll hold you to that one."

Chapter 14

Sally had a victory party at her house after the race. The crew and their wives were there. She invited Kelly, too. She wasn't sure if it was going to be a victory party or just supper, so she just ordered a deli meat tray, a veggie tray, chips and all the goodies that went with it. She had baked a couple pies, too.

Vic had the trophy and put it in the middle of the table so everyone could see it. Everyone was enjoying themselves at Sally's except Adam. He had to go home first and take a shower and change clothes. When he walked in, everyone applauded.

"Thanks everyone," Adam said running his hand through his hair. "But you know I couldn't have done it without all of you. But, thanks so much. I had so much fun." Everyone laughed at him.

"Well, I had a pretty good time myself," Hal said.

"Me, too," Vic piped up.

Everyone agreed it was a pretty good day.

Hal pulled Adam off to the side.

"Do you think you could do this two or three days in a row?" Hal asked Adam. He thought for a moment running his hand through his hair.

"Sure, I guess I could," Adam said. "As long as I get plenty of sleep the nights between." Hal nodded.

"I'd like to go to 34 and Quad Cities next weekend." Hal said. "Burlington is on Friday night, Quad Cities is on Saturday and we'd be back here for Sunday night. Do you think you could handle all that?"

"Are they all IMCA series tracks?" Adam asked him.

"Yeah," Hal said. "We're sticking with just those. I figure if we're going for point total why go to a different series."

"That's what I thought," Adam said. "Let's try it."

Monday, Adam was a celebrity as school. The kids congratulated him when they saw him in the halls. A lot of the girls batted their eyes at him which he totally ignored.

"Stupid girls," he said under his breath as he passed them.

At lunch he was talking to some of the boys when Steve Maynard sat down across from him, again.

"Not going to take her warning, are you?" He asked putting his tray down. "Nice race though."

"You know," Adam started. "I know who she is and I'm not afraid of her or worried about her."

"I heard one of the drivers saw her Sunday and refused to drive," Steve said. "That true?"

"I wouldn't know," Adam said. "I heard the same rumor but never talked to the guy. Was just one less car I had to worry about."

"So you don't think it's real?" Steve asked Adam.

"Don't know," Adam lied. "Haven't seen anything since. I was probably pretty tired that night and it was almost dark. I might have been dreaming."

"I believe it's real," Steve said very seriously. "I still think you should take warning. You're good. But are you good enough to out run a ghost?" Steve got up, picked up his tray and walked off.

Adam watched him walk away and halfway smiled.

"You ain't worried about that?" One of the other boys asked him.

"Won't do any good to worry about it," Adam said as the bell rang.

The week flew by and Adam left work at noon on Friday with his boss's blessing. The hauler had left already with the car and equipment. Sally, Vic, Hal and Adam were ready to go as soon as Adam got home. Vic was so glad that he got to take a half day off, too, in order to go with the team.

They arrived in Burlington around 3:00 and found their crew and the car. Sally went to confirm their hotel reservations and check in so they were sure to have a place to sleep after the race. She couldn't go into the pit anyway.

"How's she look?" Hal asked Colin and Randy when they walked into the garage.

"Looks great and ready to go," Randy said. "Have you ever driven this track?"

"Yeah," Adam said running his hand through his hair. "It's been a couple of years, but doesn't look like anything has changed."

"I was looking at the rules and the only changes are with some things about the cars," Bobby said. "Nothing for you to worry about."

"You just drive like you did Sunday and you'll be fine," Eddie said. Bobby nodded.

"That's what I'm planning to do," Adam said.

After Adam came back from his practice laps Colin and Randy did the same checks as always. And as always everything was fine.

"You're doing a great job with her," Hal said.

"It's a great car," Adam said rubbing his hand across the roof and leaning his head on his arm. "Way to go babe," he whispered to the car.

Adam was soon lined up for his Heat Race. He was anxious and said a real quick prayer for safety and to come out in front again while he was waiting to get started.

Adam was so surprised that there were only 8 cars in his heat race today. He had always thought that Burlington was a good place to race. Later he found out that this special Friday night race was taking away cars from other races from up north so there weren't as many cars as there usually were.

The race started without incident and Adam quickly took the lead and took control of the race. He didn't know any of the other drivers in this race but there was one guy towards the back that kept trying to bump the others to get around. He had finally bumped one too many and his right front tire flew off and slid him into the infield.

It was sad that the race had to end on a caution, but Adam still won it over ¾ of a lap ahead of his nearest competitor.

The Trophy race was a different story. There were 23 cars. Of course, again Adam was in the middle of the pack. He would have to pass just the first few cars to win and with 15 laps, this was not going to be a problem.

They took off and Adam found his groove from earlier and took over the cars before they hit the back straight away. He considered himself pretty lucky. There was Rich Uppinghouse right on his tale…drafting him. Adam didn't like the idea of other drivers drafting him, but he did his share of it, too. Every time Rich tried to shoot around him Adam dropped down. He knew Rich was getting upset with him. Then Adam did the unthinkable. He slowed down just enough that Rich had to back off.

Adam knew Rich was mad now. There weren't that many laps to go and both Rich and Adam were smart drivers. They were coming up on the pack again and were going to start lapping them very soon.

Things looked good until there was a wreck up ahead of him. Adam swerved and missed everything. The wreck caused him to lap two cars and Rich almost spun out. The yellow light came out and everyone slowed down.

"You have five laps to go," Hal called into his head piece.

"Thanks, Hal," Adam said waiting for the green flag.

It fell.

Once they were on a straight away Adam made his move and whipped around the car in front of him. There were now only three laps left and Adam pulled away. He went around the curve and down the back chute.

Barring any problems, he was going to bring another victory home for Hal. Around the first two turns, down the back chute coming up on the last curve and he saw the checkered flag ready to drop. He passed the starter and the flag fell just for him.

Adam had to remember not to scream this time. But he was so happy. He went into pit road and jumped out grabbing Hal this time and swinging the old man around.

"Put me down, you fool kid," Hal protested.

The Feature race ran pretty much the same way as the Trophy race but with three less drivers since there was the accident in the earlier race.

"That car goes faster the longer it's out there," Hal said to Randy and Colin during the race with the mic turned off.

The end of this race wasn't even close. Adam had lapped every car on the track and cruised to the checkered flag. He was still very happy with the results.

"50 points for two races," Hal said. "Not bad, kid."

Adam just smiled.

They didn't do much celebrating after this race. Hal ordered Adam and Vic directly to the hotel. The crew would take care of the car and would meet them there later. They would leave for the Quad Cities right after breakfast in the morning.

"I want to be on the road at least by 9:30," Hal told Adam and his crew. "So, no partying tonight. Everyone has to be on his toes tomorrow."

The race at the Quad Cities went pretty much like the one at Burlington. Adam won the race with his closest competitor almost a half lap behind him. With only three races under his belt, he was making a name for himself and his team.

The crew headed back to Payson immediately after the race. It was a long ride from the Quad Cities and Adam was tired. He let Eddie ride with Hal and Vic; and he lay across the back seat in the truck knowing Bobby would be home sooner than Hal. Even though he slept a couple hours, it was a restless sleep.

He dreamt about his beautiful woman again. And once again they were walking in the park hand in hand. She leaned her head on his shoulder as they were walking allowing her blond hair to fall down his arm. It felt so soft. He pulled her into his arms and was holding her face in his hand. He was getting ready to kiss her.

"Hey Adam," Bobby smacked him on the hip. "We're home."

Adam sat up in a daze. Although glad to be home, he wanted to finish his dream.

"Thanks guys," Adam said as he was heading down the street to his place. "See you tomorrow."

Bobby and Eddie waved to Adam as they unhooked the trailer and headed off to their homes. About twenty minutes later Hal pulled in with Colin, Randy and Vic. But Adam was already in bed asleep.

Sunday morning Adam was awakened by someone pounding on his door.

"I'm coming," he yelled as he crawled out of bed pulling his jeans on hopping across the kitchen.

It was Vic. Adam opened the door.

"Mom said to come down for breakfast," Vic said.

"What time is it?" Adam grumbled still pulling his fly shut.

"I think it's after 9," Vic said as he ran down the stairs. "Mom said now!"

"Mom said now," Adam repeated as he closed the door and went back to his bedroom. His bed looked so good and he was still tired. He laid across his bed just for a few more minutes. He didn't need to eat. He fell sound to sleep. Then about fifteen minutes later, Vic was back.

"Pound, pound, pound!"

"Adam, are you awake?" Vic yelled. He tried the door. It was open so he walked in. "Adam," Vic said softly as he shook Adam. "Adam wake up. You have to race this afternoon."

"I'm so tired, buddy," Adam said teasing the boy. "You race for me."

"I can't even drive yet," Vic cried. "Come on, get up." Vic tried to lift up Adam's arm. "Come on, Adam!"

Adam rolled over and sat up. Vic handed him the shirt hanging on the chair. He put it on and started to button it up.

"Don't you feel good?" Vic asked his friend.

"Yeah, I'm all right," Adam said tucking his shirt in his jeans. "I'm just tired."

They both walked down to Sally's and Adam just drank some juice instead of eating a big meal. Sally could tell that Adam wasn't his usually spunky self.

"Maybe you should sit this one out," Sally suggested.

"I'm all right," Adam said. "It's just been a long weekend."

"You going to tell Hal how tired you are?" She asked him.

"No, and neither are you," Adam said to Sally. Then turning to Vic he said, "And neither are you." Vic nodded.

After breakfast Adam lay back down on Sally's sofa and slept for another couple hours. When he woke up he felt a lot better and was ready to head over to the track. He didn't know that Hal had stopped by and saw he was sleeping and left without him. After all, they didn't need him until race time anyway.

Sally, Vic and Adam got to the track just before noon. Adam and Vic went to the pit and found Hal and the crew right away.

"Feeling better, son?" Hal asked Adam when they walked up. "I need an alert driver today."

"I'm fine," Adam said. "Just needed some sleep."

"Are you ready to take her out?" Colin asked handing Adam his jumpsuit and boots.

"Give me five minutes and I will be," he replied with a smile.

Adam sat on the wall of the pit and slipped into his jump suit. Vic helped him on with his boots then handed him his helmet. Adam climbed into the car, got buckled in tight and was ready for his practice laps. He hadn't even got out of pit road when he blew a tire. Bobby, Eddie and Dusty ran the fifty feet to him and pushed the car back to where it started.

"I sure hope this isn't a sign of things to come today," Adam said as he sat in the car waiting for them to change the tire.

When they let the car down off the jack, Colin gave Adam the signal to try it again. He drove it slowly down pit road and onto the track. It felt good. He couldn't tell the difference with the new tire. He took a few laps at a decent speed and brought her back in.

"Any problems?" Randy asked with Colin and Hal waiting for an answer.

"Not that I could tell," Adam said. "She felt great and ready to take on all comers."

All the races went fine until the Feature. Adam and Rich Uppinghouse started out side by side. Adam knew he was going to be his biggest completion. Rich looked over at Adam and gave a thumbs up and Adam reciprocated. They may have been friends off the course, but not now.

The race was on. Rich flew out ahead of Adam as did two other cars.

"What the hell!" Hal cried not realizing his mic was on.

"It's just the beginning, old man," Adam said.

Adam passed the other two cars and was closing in on Rich. He passed him on the back straight away and flew ahead of him as if he caught Rich asleep at the wheel. But Rich recovered from the surprise and caught up quickly to Adam. It was a two man race. The rest of the field was so far behind them they could play with each other. Rich passed Adam and Adam let him go ahead just enough that he could tuck behind Rich and draft him for a lap or two. The crowd was going crazy.

"Quit jacking around!" Hal called into Adam's ear piece.

"Yes, sir," Adam said that as he shot around Rich and with the slingshot burst of power almost caught up with the pack and started to lap the cars. Rich pounded on the steering wheel of his car. Adam was so far ahead of him now and in traffic and there were only a couple laps left. Rich doubted there was going to be time to catch up to Adam. He was mad at himself now but he had to keep his head.

Adam passed the starter with the white flag. He smiled. He drove cautiously letting the cars stay alongside of him and in front of him.

Rich was behind him with the other cars. He saw the checkered flag raised for him. And down it came. He had won his fourth race in two weekends.

After the race the crew was standing around the car celebrating and talking. Rich came over to congratulate Adam.

"Way to go, kid," Rich said as he extended his hand.

"Thanks," Adam said.

""So our ghost story isn't scaring you off," Rich said as he sat on the pit wall.

"Naw," Adam said. "I don't think she's going to bother me. If anything, looks like she's bringing me luck." Adam smiled at Rich.

"Maybe it's not you she wants," Rich said.

"Maybe," Adam said.

"Well, good luck, pal," Rich said shaking Adam's hand again as he walked off.

"You, too, buddy," Adam said to Rich.

Adam was so glad when school was out and he didn't have to work. Hal had a lot of racing planned for them and they went to Donnellson, Iowa, back to Burlington and the Quad Cities several times. But he still liked his home track the best.

Adam was getting quite famous and was drawing quite a few competitors trying to show up the young driver. Very few of them could even stay close to him and Rich Uppinghouse from Payson was still his closest competitor. Rich and Adam stayed very close in the point count, too, staying a matter of ten to twenty points away from each other all summer. No one else was even close.

Chapter 15

It was late August and the stands were full watching one of the tightest point races the IMCA had seen in several years. Rich and Adam were separated by a mere 8 points and there were only five weekends left to the season. Rich had won a few races during the summer but Adam had taken most of them away from Rich at the last minute.

They had a friendly rivalry, but once they were on the track the friendship was gone. Tonight Adam won the Heat Race which put him nine points ahead. Rich knew he needed every point. He was going to pull out everything he had, everything he was taught from his late father to beat Adam.

When they were sitting in their cars waiting for the feature, Rich put his head down on the steering wheel and said quietly, "Dad, this one's for you."

Once again Rich and Adam were taking the lead from each other. First Adam had it then Rich had it. Back and forth. It was one of the best races of the season. Adam finally pulled away leaving Rich in the dust.

The car was performing the best it had done all season. Adam was streaming along the straight away and drifting so smoothly around the curves. He was confident he had this race won. There were two laps to go and no one was even close to him…Rich was even about a half lap behind him. But, he didn't let up because he knew what a split second could cost him in one of these races. Around he went and got the white flag indicating just one more lap and he had it in his pocket. The first and second curves were smooth and the back straight away was nice. But then the car just died. The engine continued to purr but Adam had no control over it. He saw the wall getting close on the third curve and felt the thud at the fourth.

The crowd stood up as the yellow light went on and the cars passed Adam's totally destroyed car. No one saw Rich receive the checkered flag and win the race. Hal and his crew were at the pit wall. Vic stood at Hal's side holding up the wavering old man. The crowd was silent. The roar of the engines slowly dissipated as the cars drove down pit road and into the garages. The ambulance, fire truck and tow truck were at the crash site before the last race car had left the track. Everyone held their breath, hoping, praying that Adam would be all right.

Sally ran down to pit road to be with the crew.

"There she is," Vic said softly looking out toward the crash. "She's helping him out of the car." Tears were trickling down his cheeks.

Sally was the only one who heard his soft words. She looked over at him and put her arm around his waist.

"Is it Shari Rose, Vic?" Sally quietly asked her son. He nodded.

"She come for Adam," Vic whispered wiping his cheeks with the back of his hand.

There was a gasp from the entire crowd. Sally couldn't believe her eyes.

"Oh Mother of Jesus," Hal said crossing himself then rubbing his eyes.

People could not believe what they were experiencing. The entire crowd saw the spirit of Shari Rose helping Adam out of the mangled black beauty 350 stock car. He stood up, pulled off his helmet and dropped it to the ground.

"Thanks, ma'am," Adam said to Shari Rose. She simply smiled at him.

Adam glanced over his shoulder to the ruined car. Through the shattered windshield a pale, blood splattered hand caught his eye. "That ring," he thought casually, "it's just like mine". Suddenly he froze then turned slowly to face the wreck. The ring didn't just look like his but was his. Adam was gazing at the lifeless shell that he once was. Adam, filled with sadness, realized he was dead.

He looked back at Shari Rose who nodded. He looked toward pit road seeing Hal, Vic and Sally. He needed to tell them good-bye. He tried to walk toward them but Shari Rose put her hand on Adam's arm.

"They know," she finally said to him. Adam really looked at her for the first time.

She was beautiful, but she didn't look exactly like her pictures he had seen. She was prettier than that. She was the woman he had been waiting for all his life; the one that he had been dreaming about. He reached up and touched her face. It was so soft. He leaned down and gently kissed her.

Shari Rose took Adam's hand and they walked off the track and into the woods.

The obituary for Adam was longer than the write up for the race. So many people wanted to do something special to honor him, but his body was sent back to his family. So, Scott decided to have a memorial at the track. The stands were filled and people were standing in the infield, sitting on the walls, standing in pit road and just about everywhere they could find a place. The State Police were called just to direct traffic.

The service consisted of a few Bible verses and some words from the Pastor of the Congregational Church. Rich represented his racing pals and passed along stories and of course, Hal had his oration to give.

During the service one of the EMT's that was working the day of the accident made his way over to Kelly.

"Hey girl," Jake said as he gave her a little hug. "You doing OK?"

"Yeah, thanks Jake," Kelly said moving a little closer to Sally so he could sit down.

"I wanted to bring something to you I found the night of the crash but I've been kind of putting it off," Jake said lowering his head. "I can't explain it"

"What is it?" Kelly asked as Jake shoved his hand into his pocket pulling out something in his fist. He grabbed Kelly's hand and put his fist into it, slowly opening it, letting the cross on the chain fall out of his hand into hers.

Kelly pulled her hand away so quickly the cross almost fell out of her hand.

"Oh my God!" Kelly cried. "I thought this was gone for good."

"It's weird, Kel," Jake said. "When I was done with my shift, I was pretty upset. I went on home and was getting ready to take a shower. I usually just empty my pockets and toss my clothes in the laundry basket. Anyway, I just threw my pants on the chair. This fell out of the pocket onto the floor. I have no idea how it got in there." Jake had tears in his eyes. "I remembered Shari Rose always wore it. I remembered you said it wasn't on her body when she had her wreck.

I don't understand how I got it."

"You were busy the other night so you didn't see everything that went on," Kelly said.

"You mean, I didn't see Shari Rose come get Adam," Jake said. "I saw them disappear into the woods. If I hadn't seen it I wouldn't have believed it."

"I think this is a sign saying that everything is all right now," Kelly said. Jake nodded.

"Mom," Vic pulled on Sally's sleeve. "Do you see them?" He whispered as he pointed towards the woods.

Sally tried to focus toward the woods at the far end of the track. She saw the couple sitting deep in the woods watching as if guarding the track now. She smiled.

"I do," Sally whispered. "I do see them, Victor."

"They look happy, Mom," Vic said with a smile. "Shari Rose isn't crying anymore."

www.ingramcontent.com/pod-product-compliance
Ingram Content Group UK Ltd.
Pitfield, Milton Keynes, MK11 3LW, UK
UKHW040601210726
13854UKWH00008B/1659